I0007980

Building macOS Apps With SwiftUI

A Practical Learning Guide

Grace Huang

Table of Contents

INTRODUCTION

Introduced in 2019, SwiftUI is a user interface toolkit that let you create applications with the power of the programming language Swift for all Apple platforms, including iOS, tvOS, watchOS, and macOS.

Before the launch of SwiftUI, developers had to use platform-specific UI frameworks to develop user interfaces, for example, AppKit for macOS apps, TVUIKit for tvOS, and WatchKit for watchOS apps. SwiftUI becomes the one unified UI framework for building user interfaces for all Apple devices.

This book will primarily focus on building macOS apps with SwiftUI, including both coding and releasing apps. Some details for releasing apps on different platforms (iOS, macOS, tvOS, and WatchOS) may differ, so I believe a single focus on macOS development will bring more clarity and avoid confusion.

This book will also touch upon the basics of SwiftUI, which can be potentially shared for other platforms.

I first published an article on Medium about my playbook for macOS app development, which enabled me to quickly turn ideas into apps, and publish them in apps. It received quite a lot of views and shares. This motivated me to write this book with practical examples, so readers who are new to macOS app development can learn, practice, and publish apps hopefully by the end of the book.

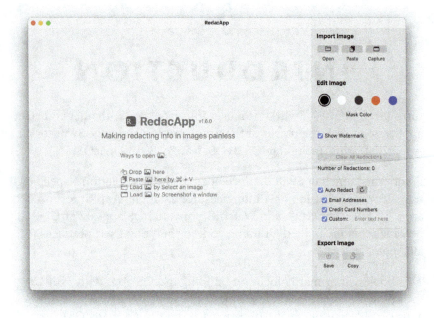

Figure 0-1 One of my apps RedacApp was built with SwiftUI.

END GOAL

Once you have finished reading this book, you should be able to create macOS apps on your own and publish them to your users. Building a macOS app will no longer be a mystery to you. You will be familiar with the end-to-end process.

STRUCTURE

> *"Learning is an active process. We learn by doing. Only knowledge that is used sticks in your mind."*— Dale Carnegie, How to Stop Worrying and Start Living

In light of this guiding principle by Dale Carnegie, this book prioritizes doing and then goes into the details later.

The book is structured into 4 parts. Each part consists of multiple chapters.

Part 1

The first part is getting you ready for the development:

- Chapter 1: Getting Started

Part 2

The second part is a walkthrough of multiple macOS projects. It guides you to create these applications from scratch, using SwiftUI.

The chapters are:

- Chapter 2: Building A Note-taking App

- Chapter 3: Building A Windowless Screenshot App

- Chapter 4: Building A Photo Fetching App

Part 3

The third part is a deep dive into macOS development and SwiftUI basics. Why place the part of basics after the projects? It is counter-intuitive, but we learn better by doing first (building the projects). You may have questions along the way. This part will be the place to answer them in detail.

- Chapter 5: macOS Development and SwiftUI Basics

Part 4

The fourth part is about preparation for the app release.

The chapters are:

- Chapter 6: Preparing For Launch

- Chapter 7: App Store

- Chapter 8: Self-Distribution

PREREQUISITES

1. A Mac computer that can run Xcode

2. Internet access

3. $99 for Apple Developer Program

Yes, every macOS and iOS developer has to pay $99 annually to develop and distribute apps. I will explain this in detail later in the book.

ASSUMPTIONS

This book assumes that you are new to macOS app development with SwiftUI, not necessarily new to programming in general. If you have prior programming experience in other languages, it should be easier to follow the steps in the book.

This book focuses on using SwiftUI to build macOS apps but does not dive deep into the Swift language. Throughout the book, tips for Swift will be mentioned.

In addition, the latest Xcode version at the time of writing is 14. All the examples and screenshots are based on Xcode 14. If you have earlier or later Xcode versions, please expect some differences. I will try my best to bring the book up to date as time goes on.

All the code in this book is written in Swift 5. If you build your project with an earlier or later Swift Language Version, please expect some differences.

FORMATS

When you are following along with the projects in the book, here are some visual signals that can guide you.

- ✽ : this means a step. You can follow it throughout the book for the actionable steps, and skim through other parts to save time.

- ❖ Tip: this means information related that may be helpful to you, but it may not be immediately useful in the context.

Bold text often corresponds to keywords in the figures and code.

GETTING BOOK UPDATES

I will do my best to keep the book up to date with the latest versions of Xcode and SwiftUI. To receive the latest updates on the book, subscribe to my mailing list by sending an email to higracehuang@gmail.com.

CODE EXAMPLES

You can get a copy of the source code here: https://github.com/higracehuang

SUGGESTIONS

Your feedback will always be appreciated. If there is anything unclear or typos in this book, please feel free to contact me via any of the following ways:

- Email: higracehuang@gmail.com

- Twitter: https://twitter.com/imgracehuang

- LinkedIn: https://www.linkedin.com/in/lghuang/

Now, let's cut to the chase!

CHAPTER 1: GETTING STARTED

If you have done iOS development in the past, the steps discussed in this chapter will be very similar. Feel free to skip this chapter and move on to the next chapter!

MAC COMPUTER

To develop a macOS app, you can use a regular MacBook, MacBook Air, or iMac. It does not matter.

However, newer models may have more powerful processors. With them, you'll see a dramatic time reduction in build times, hence faster development on Xcode.

INSTALL XCODE

✖ Open the app **App Store** on your Mac

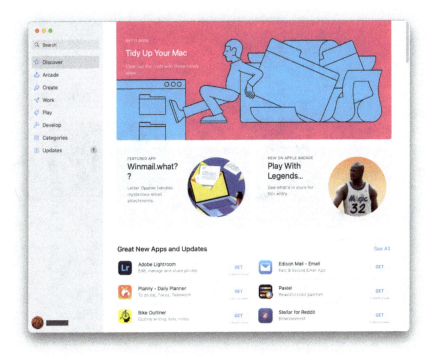

Figure1-1 The App Store app

✖ Search **Xcode** in App Store.

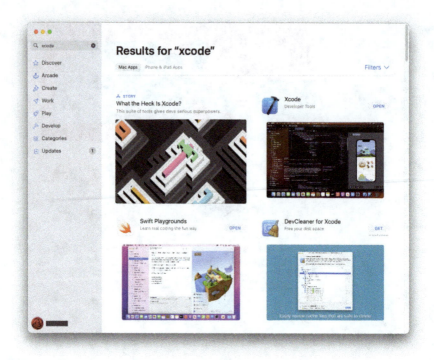

Figure 1-2 Search results of App Store

✖ You should find **Xcode** in the search results. Click **Get**. In the screenshot above, the button shows **Open**, because the Xcode has been installed. If you have never installed Xcode, the button should show **Get**.

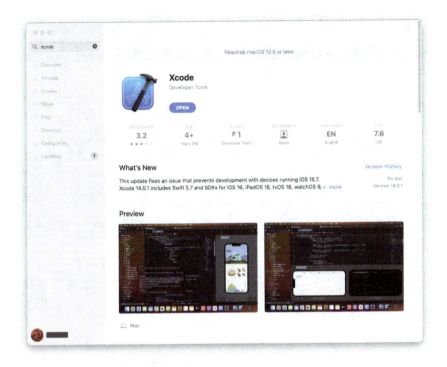

Figure 1-3 App detail page of Xcode

The installation may take a while, because the size of Xcode is 7.6 GB at the time of writing. While waiting, make yourself a cup of coffee or tea. You deserve it!

Make sure you have reliable internet during the download and installation.

APPLE DEVELOPER PROGRAM MEMBERSHIP

To develop macOS or iOS, we will need to enroll in the Apple Developer Program. Membership includes access to beta OS releases, advanced app capabilities, and tools needed to develop, test, and distribute apps.

At the time of writing, it costs $99 for individuals and organizations per year.

You may wonder, if you are not ready to publish this app to App Store, do you still need to pay $99 immediately? The answer is no. You can build it on your Mac computer. However, once you are ready to release, you will need to be in the program.

❖ Tip

Do you know you can develop multiple apps (both macOS and iOS) with the $99 per year? Even though this upfront cost seems like a lot to some people, you can get more benefits out of this program if you plan to develop multiple apps.

✖ Go to https://developer.apple.com/programs/, and click **Enroll**. It will lead you to the enrollment process.

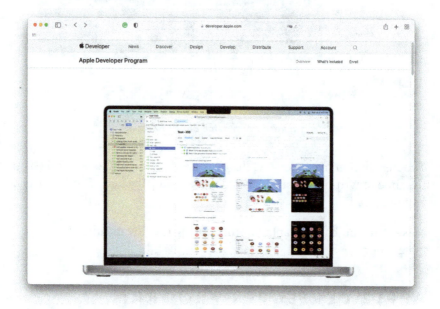

Figure 1-4 Apple Developer Program website

✖ Once you have finished the signup process and paid the annual fee, you will receive a confirmation email like the following.

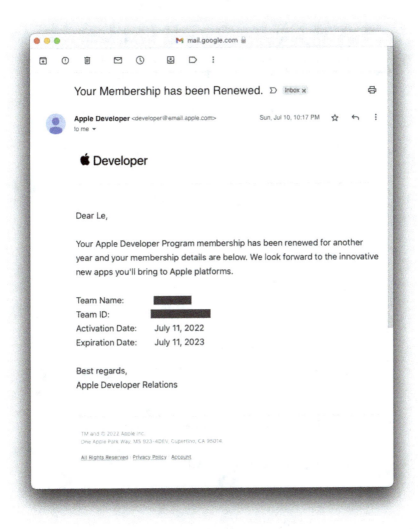

Figure 1-5 Email confirmation of Apple Developer Program

Ready to create something? Let's go!

CHAPTER 2: BUILDING A NOTE-TAKING APP

In this chapter, we will build a very simple note-taking app together:

Figure 2-1 The Note-taking app we are building

By building this, we will get familiar with:

- The process to create a macOS app in general

- How to use Core Data for local storage

- Basics of SwiftUI

REQUIREMENTS FOR THIS APP

This note-taking app needs to have the following features:

- A user can view all the notes

- A user can edit any note

- The note persists after the app quits

CREATING A MACOS APP PROJECT

At this point, Xcode is downloaded and installed on your Mac computer, and we are ready to create an app.

✖ Open **Xcode** app. On the left pane, you have a few options for starting a project. On the right pane are the existing projects. Assuming this is the new time you are using Xcode, the right pan should be empty. Let's choose the option **Create a new Xcode project**.

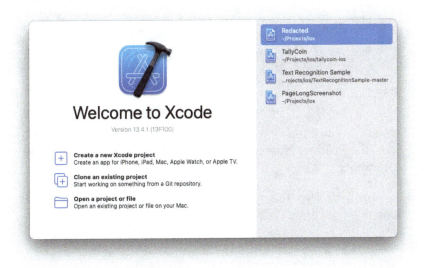

Figure 2-2 Create a new Xcode project

✖ Choose **macOS** in the top menu, and choose **App** in **Application**.

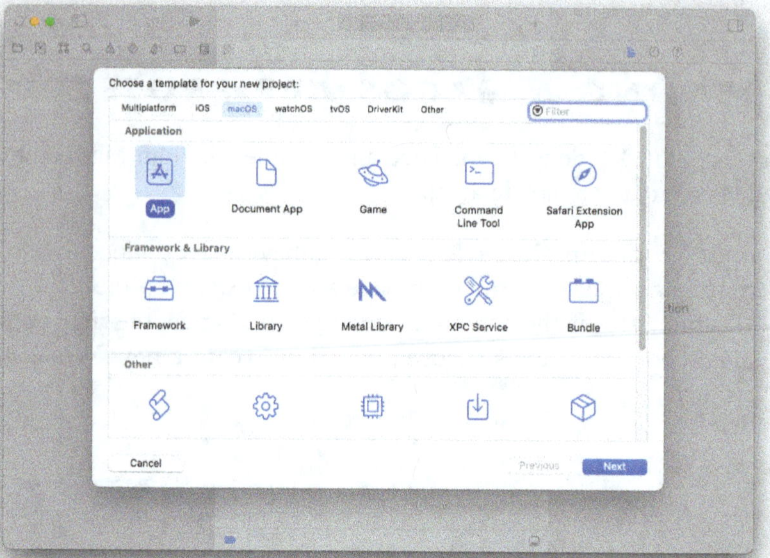

Figure 2-3 Select macOS > App

- Enter the **Product Name**. In this example, we will just simply call it **notetaking**.
- For now, let's keep **Team** as **None**. We will talk about it later in the book.
- Enter the **Organization Identifier**. In this example, we will use **com.unicornproject**. As you type it, you can quickly notice the **Bundle Identifier** is formed as **com.unicornproject.notetaking**.
- Choose **SwiftUI** as **Interface**, and **Swift** as the **Language**.

❖ Tip

Swift is the programming language we are using to build the app. Before Swift was the main programming language, it was Objective-C.

Swift has a simpler syntax than Objective-C. According to an article by Fast Company[1], when the second largest ride-sharing company Lyft rewrote the iOS code from Objective-C to Swift, the code base size went down to less than a third of the original size.

Swift also offers better memory management. As stated by Apple[2], Swift is 2.6 times faster than Objective-C.

SwiftUI is a whole set of tools that gives us images, buttons, form elements, and many other common UI controls. With all these tools, SwiftUI creates a piece of UI, called View.

 Turn on **Use Core Data**. We will use this feature later in the project. Then click **Next**.

Figure 2-4 Fill in the information for the new project

❖ Tip

---

[1] https://www.fastcompany.com/3050266/lyft-goes-swift-how-and-why-it-rewrote-its-app-from-scratch-in-apples-new-lang

[2] https://www.apple.com/in/swift/

A **Bundle Identifier** is used to identify this particular app. An **Organization Identifier** is used to identify the company or individual that develops this project.

For example, for the Screenshot app in macOS, the **Bundle Identifier** is **com.apple.screencapture**. In this case, the **Organization Identifier** is com.apple. The Project Name is **screencapture**.

❖ Tip

Core Data is a framework that you can use to manage data object graphs in your application. It is frequently used for local data storage.

In our note-taking app, we will need to store the note on the device. We will dive into Core Data even more later.

You can also choose not to turn on Core Data now if you are not sure whether your app will use Core Data. If you later find out it is needed, you can still set it up later.

✖ Choose the directory under which you would like to save the project.

Figure 2-5 Select where to save the project

✖ Make sure to turn on **Create Git repository on my Mac**. A git local repository will be initialized when the project is created. In this example, let's save the note-taking project under the directory **apps**.

■ Click **Create**, to finally create the project. Xcode will create a basic app for you.

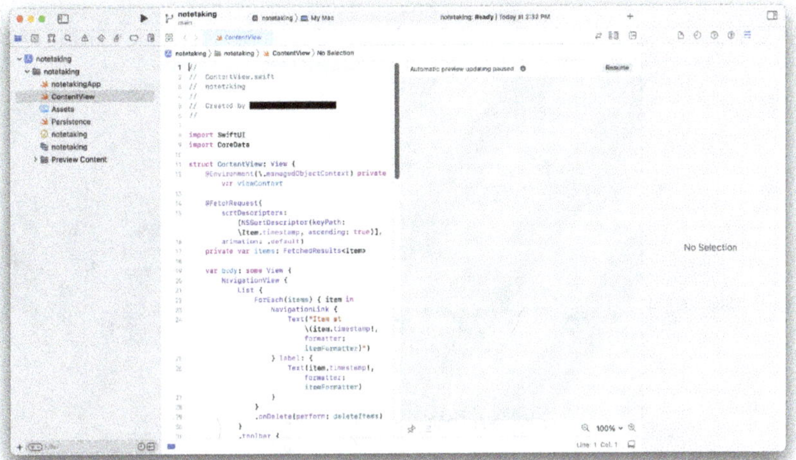

Figure 2-6 Code generated by Xcode

At this point, the code we have so far is also committed to your local git history.

PLAYING WITH THE APP

Now we have a working app! Let's try it.

■ Click the ▶ button on the left pane of Xcode, to run the app. Once the build is complete, you will see a functioning app.

❖ Tip

Throughout the book, we will frequently mention running the app by clicking the ▶ button, to verify no build errors.

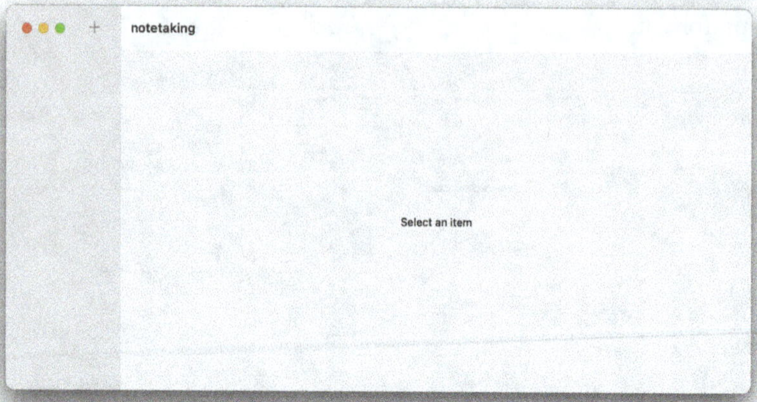

Figure 2-7 How the app works initially

In this app, you can see:

- A + sign on the top
- A left pane
- A right pane

Click the + sign, and an entry will be created on the left pane. When you click on the new entry, the right pane will be updated with new content.

Figure 2-8 When clicking on the right, it shows the basic details

It is already very cool, isn't it? With this, we are empowered to add more functionalities on top of this base code. Let's go!

DIVING DEEP INTO CONTENTVIEW CODE

In Xcode, click to open **ContentView.swift**.

ContentView.swift

```swift
import SwiftUI
import CoreData

struct ContentView: View {
  @Environment(\.managedObjectContext) private var viewContext

  @FetchRequest(
    sortDescriptors: [
      NSSortDescriptor(keyPath: \Item.timestamp, ascending: true)
    ],
    animation: .default)
  private var items: FetchedResults<Item>

  var body: some View {
    NavigationView {
      List {
        ForEach(items) { item in
          NavigationLink {
            Text("Item at \(item.timestamp!, formatter: itemFormatter)")
          } label: {
            Text(item.timestamp!, formatter: itemFormatter)
          }
        }
```

```swift
                    .onDelete(perform: deleteItems)
                }
                .toolbar {
                    ToolbarItem {
                        Button(action: addItem) {
                            Label("Add Item", systemImage: "plus")
                        }
                    }
                }
                Text("Select an item")
            }
        }

    private func addItem() {
        withAnimation {
            let newItem = Item(context: viewContext)
            newItem.timestamp = Date()

            do {
                try viewContext.save()
            } catch {
                let nsError = error as NSError
                fatalError("Unresolved error \(nsError), \(nsError.userInfo)")
            }
        }
    }

    private func deleteItems(offsets: IndexSet) {
        withAnimation {
            offsets.map { items[$0] }.forEach(viewContext.delete)

            do {
                try viewContext.save()
            } catch {
                let nsError = error as NSError
                fatalError("Unresolved error \(nsError), \(nsError.userInfo)")
            }
        }
    }
}

private let itemFormatter: DateFormatter = {
    let formatter = DateFormatter()
    formatter.dateStyle = .short
    formatter.timeStyle = .medium
    return formatter
}()

struct ContentView_Previews: PreviewProvider {
    static var previews: some View {
        ContentView().environment(
            \.managedObjectContext,
            PersistenceController.preview.container.viewContext)
    }
}
```

Let's take a look at how it works.

Previews

In this file, you can see two structs: **ContentView** and **ContentView_Previews**.

ContentView.swift

```swift
struct ContentView: View { … }

struct ContentView_Previews: PreviewProvider { … }
```

ContentView struct describes the content and layout. The app will rely on this definition.

ContentView_Previews describes how to show the preview (a.k.a., canvas) for ContentView. When the app is running, it does not run this part at all. It is very helpful when you are developing.

Figure 2-9 Preview of the app

Whenever the view is updated, without running the app, you can easily see what it looks like in the Preview.

❖ Tip

If the Preview is stopped during development, you can reload the preview window by pressing **Option-Command-P**.

❖ Tip

If you prefer not not to the preview, you can simply remove the struct **ContentView_Previews**.

To hide the **Preview** window, you can press **Option-Command-Return**, or check off **Canvas** in the **Editor** menu.

Environment Variable

```
@Environment(\.managedObjectContext) private var viewContext
```

Managed Object Context is used here to facilitate saving and deleting Core Data. However, fetching Core Data does not need Managed Object Context.

In this view, **manageObjectContext** is passed as an environment variable. But where does it get passed? It is defined in **Persistence.swift**, and then referenced in **notetakingApp.swift**, and eventually read in **ContentView.swift** by adding an **@Environment** property.

Persistence.swift

```
struct PersistenceController {
  static let shared = PersistenceController()
  …
  let container: NSPersistentContainer
  …
}
```

notetakingApp.swift

```
import SwiftUI

@main
struct notetakingApp: App {
  let persistenceController = PersistenceController.shared

  var body: some Scene {
    WindowGroup {
      ContentView()
        .environment(
          \.managedObjectContext,
          persistenceController.container.viewContext)
    }
  }
}
```

@Environment is one way to manage shared resources in SwiftUI. We will discuss this with other alternatives in Chapter 5.

FetchRequest

When the ContentView is created, it will fetch a collection of items from the Core Data persistence store. The results will be solved by the ascending timestamp.

ContentView.swift

```
@FetchRequest(sortDescriptors: [
  NSSortDescriptor(keyPath: \Item.timestamp, ascending: true)
], animation: .default)
```

NavigationView

The foundation of the **ContentView** is this **NavigationView**.
NavigationView is a user interface where the user clicks on a
NavigationLink on one pane, and the destination of the
NavigationLink will display on the other pane.

ContentView.swift

```
var body: some View {
  NavigationView {
    List {
      ForEach(items) { item in
        NavigationLink {
          Text("Item at \(item.timestamp!, formatter: itemFormatter)")
        } label: {
          Text(item.timestamp!, formatter: itemFormatter)
        }
      }.onDelete(perform: deleteItems)
    }.toolbar {
      ToolbarItem {
        Button(action: addItem) {
          Label("Add Item", systemImage: "plus")
        }
      }
    }
    Text("Select an item")
  }
}
```

Inside the **NavigationView**, a List hosts a collection of
NavigationLinks.

Adding and Deleting Items

Two functions handle the data transactions: **addItem()** and
deleteItems().

Item is an entity in Core Data. **Item()** creates an entry of the entity
Item, and will be saved to Core Data. This happens when addItem is
called.

ContentView.swift

```
private func addItem() {
  withAnimation {
    let newItem = Item(context: viewContext)
    newItem.timestamp = Date()
```

```
  do {
    try viewContext.save()
  } catch {
    let nsError = error as NSError
    fatalError("Unresolved error \(nsError), \(nsError.userInfo)")
  }
 }
}
```

Similarly, given a set of indexes of items, **deleteItems()** deletes them from the Core Data.

ContentView.swift

```
private func deleteItems(offsets: IndexSet) {
  withAnimation {
    offsets.map { items[$0] }.forEach(viewContext.delete)

    do {
      try viewContext.save()
    } catch {
      let nsError = error as NSError
      fatalError("Unresolved error \(nsError), \(nsError.userInfo)")
    }
  }
}
```

Date Formatter

The **itemFormatter** defines how timestamp is being formatted.

In the code, the date format is defined as short, so an example of the output is 3/28/17 - mm/dd/yy.

The time format is defined as medium, so an example of the output is 1:26:32 PM.

ContentView.swift

```
private let itemFormatter: DateFormatter = {
  let formatter = DateFormatter()
  formatter.dateStyle = .short
  formatter.timeStyle = .medium
  return formatter
}()
```

For both time and date, they are other types of formats. You can change to fit your needs.

DESIGNING THE DATA MODEL

At this point, we know how the generated code works. We can make changes on top of it to make this app into a note-taking app.

Current Data Model

In the Project Navigator, click the **notetaking.xcdatamodeld**.

Figure 2-10 Core data setup of the app

Currently, it only has one entity called **Item**, and the entity **Item** has one attribute called **timestamp**.

Requirements

In the note-taking app, for each note entry, we will need the following:

- Title: String, Required

- Content: String, Optional

- Creation timestamp: Date, Required

- Update timestamp: Date, Required

Adding a New Entity

With the above requirements, let's configure the Core Data.

✖ Click **Add Entity**. A new entity called **Entity** will be created.

✖ Double click the entity **Entity**, to rename **Entity** To **NoteEntry**.

✖ Under **Attributes**, click + to add **content** as **String**, **title** as **String**, **createdAt** as **Date** and **updatedAt** as **Date**.

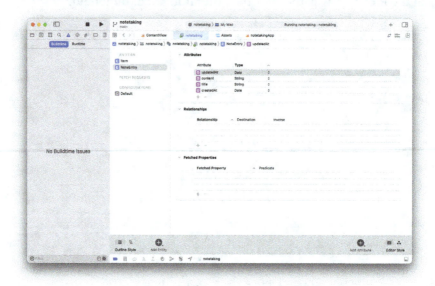

Figure 2-11 Adding all attributes in Core Data

✖ For the attributes **title** and **createdAt**, use the data model inspector (choose **View** > **Inspectors** > **Show Data Model Inspector**) to configure them to be not **Optional**.

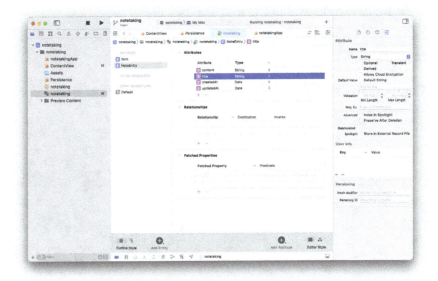

Figure 2-12 Uncheck Optional in the right pane

✖ Run the app. The build should be successful because we haven't added anything to the code logic yet.

READING CORE DATA FROM CONTENTVIEW

Creating a FetchRequest for NoteEntry

✖ Similar to the **Item FetchedRequest**, create another for NoteEntry. In addition, we want to sort the entries by the creation timestamp.

ContentView.swift

```
@FetchRequest(
    sortDescriptors: [NSSortDescriptor(keyPath: \NoteEntry.createdAt,
ascending: true)], animation: .default)
private var noteEntries: FetchedResults<NoteEntry>
```

✖ Run the app now. It should have no errors. The UI should still look like it was before. The app is pulling note entries from Core Data, but it has no record yet.

Reading From NoteEntry

Now, we can read the note entries from the **FetchRequest** that we just did.

■ Replace the body with the following:

ContentView.swift

```
var body: some View {
  NavigationView {
    List {
      ForEach(noteEntries) { noteEntry in
        if let title = noteEntry.title,
           let content = noteEntry.content,
           let updatedAt = noteEntry.updatedAt {
          NavigationLink {
            Text(content)
          } label: {
            Text(title)
            Text(updatedAt, formatter: itemFormatter)
          }
        }
      }
      .onDelete(perform: deleteItems)
    }
    .toolbar {
      ToolbarItem {
        Button(action: addItem) {
          Label("Add Note", systemImage: "plus")
        }
      }
    }
    Text("Select a note")
  }
}
```

Notice the **if** and **let** statement wraps around **NavigationLink**? Let me explain.

The attributes of an entity are optional by default. Even though some of them are defined as non-optional in Core Data, the generated attributes are still optional in Swift language.

Therefore, when we want to display the attributes in views, we need to unwrap the optional and get the value.

We have 3 options to unwrap the optionals: optional binding, unconditional unwrapping, and using the nil-coalescing operator.

Optional Binding

```
if let title = noteEntry.title,
   let content = noteEntry.content,
   let updatedAt = noteEntry.updatedAt {
  NavigationLink {
    Text(content)
  } label: {
    Text(title)
```

```
    Text(updatedAt, formatter: itemFormatter)
  }
}
```

Unconditional Unwrapping

```
ForEach(noteEntries) { noteEntry in
  NavigationLink {
    Text(noteEntry.content!)
  } label: {
    Text(noteEntry.title!)
    Text(noteEntry.updatedAt!, formatter: itemFormatter)
  }
}
```

If you are sure that the attribute is never nil, you can simply use the forced unwrap operator (postfix !) to get the value directly.

Be cautious when using the forced unwrap operator. If it happens to be nil, the app may crash.

Using the nil-coalescing operator

```
NavigationLink {
  Text(noteEntry.content ?? "")
} label: {
  Text(noteEntry.title ?? "Untitled")
  Text(noteEntry.updatedAt ?? Date(), formatter: itemFormatter)
}
```

Use the nil-coalescing operator (??) to supply a default value in case the **Optional** instance is nil.

Optional Binding is my favorite of all at most times. It is safe and structured easily. You can choose the option that fits your use case.

❖ Tip

A quick way to format your code properly is to highlight the code and press **Control-I**.

It is very handy when you need to change a lot of code all of sudden. You don't have to worry about the correct indentation at the time of change. You will only need to format afterward.

ADDING NEW ENTRY TO NOTEENTRY ENTITY

We now update the addItem function to update NoteEntries, instead of Items.

■ Rename all of the occurrences of addItem to addNoteEntry.

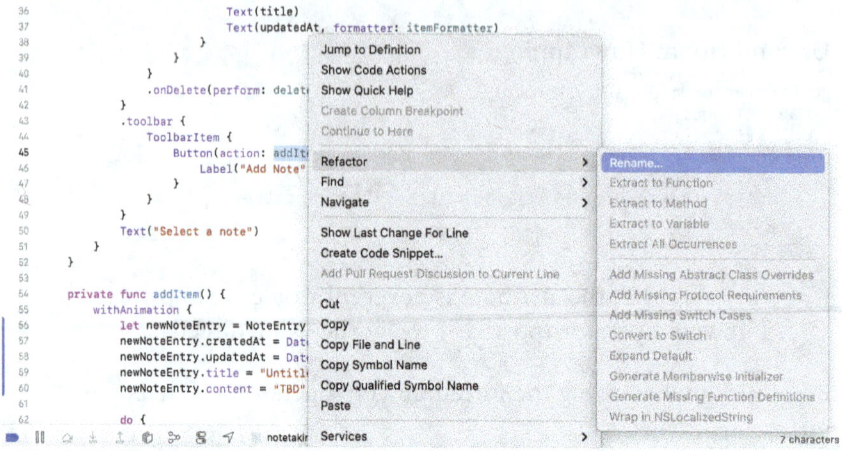

Figure 2-13 Highlight the variable addItem, right click to bring up the context menu. Choose Refactor > Rename...

■ Update the function **addNoteEntry** with the following code.

ContentView.swift

```swift
private func addNoteEntry() {
  withAnimation {
    /// Create a new object of NoteEntry
    let newNoteEntry = NoteEntry(context: viewContext)

    /// Fill the object with some data.
    /// We will update here later.
    newNoteEntry.createdAt = Date()
    newNoteEntry.updatedAt = Date()
    newNoteEntry.title = "Untitled"
    newNoteEntry.content = "TBD"

    do {
      try viewContext.save()
    } catch {
      let nsError = error as NSError
      fatalError("Unresolved error \(nsError), \(nsError.userInfo)")
    }
  }
}
```

■ Now, let's run it.

Click the + button, it should create a note entry. Click on the title of the new entry, it should display TBD as expected.

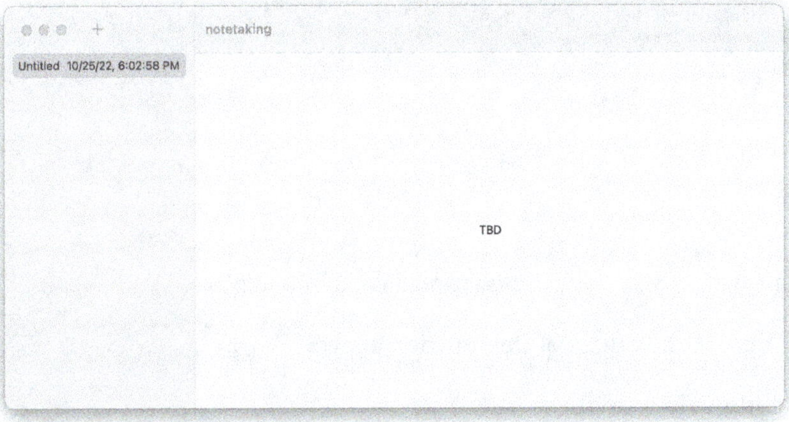

Figure 2-14 The left pane shows a combination of the title and createdAt.

Wonderful progress! We now can confirm the app is reading the NoteEntries entity we just created.

UPDATING NOTE ENTRIES

We want to have our values for note title and note content, rather than constant values like **Untitled** and **TBD**.

Refactor the transaction functions

Before we start to change the view, let's clean up the code and do some preparation.

- Move **addNoteEntry**() from **ContentView.swift** to **Persistence.swift**, as one of the members in **PersistenceController**. Because **viewContext** will be missing in the new file, we also add let viewContext = container.viewContext.

Persistence.swift

```
struct PersistenceController {
  static let shared = PersistenceController()

  ...

  func addNoteEntry() {
    let viewContext = container.viewContext
    let newNoteEntry = NoteEntry(context: viewContext)
    newNoteEntry.createdAt = Date()
```

```
    newNoteEntry.updatedAt = Date()
    newNoteEntry.title = "Untitled"
    newNoteEntry.content = "TBD"

    do {
      try viewContext.save()
    } catch {
      let nsError = error as NSError
      fatalError("Unresolved error \(nsError), \(nsError.userInfo)")
    }
  }
}
```

This way, we can keep transactional code in one place.

- Update the callers of the function above.

ContentView.swift

```
ToolbarItem {
  Button(action: PersistenceController.shared.addNoteEntry) {
    Label("Add Note", systemImage: "plus")
  }
}
```

- Delete **deleteItems()** and its reference. At this moment, we don't need the functionality.

Delete the function definition:

```
private func deleteItems(offsets: IndexSet) {
  withAnimation {
    offsets.map { items[$0] }.forEach(viewContext.delete)

    do {
      try viewContext.save()
    } catch {
      let nsError = error as NSError
      fatalError("Unresolved error \(nsError), \(nsError.userInfo)")
    }
  }
}
```

Delete the reference:

```
.onDelete(perform: deleteItems)
```

- Delete the **FetchRequest** for Item. We don't use the entity Item anymore. We only use **NoteEntry**. Delete the following from the code.

ContentView.swift

```
@FetchRequest(
  sortDescriptors: [
    NSSortDescriptor(
      keyPath: \Item.timestamp,
      ascending: true)
  ],
  animation: .default)
```

```
private var items: FetchedResults<Item>
```

After the code cleanup, the ContentView is a lot cleaner and should look like this:

ContentView.swift

```swift
import SwiftUI
import CoreData

struct ContentView: View {
  @Environment(\.managedObjectContext) private var viewContext

  @FetchRequest(
    sortDescriptors: [
      NSSortDescriptor(keyPath: \NoteEntry.createdAt, ascending: true)
    ],
    animation: .default)
  private var noteEntries: FetchedResults<NoteEntry>

  var body: some View {
    NavigationView {
      List {
        ForEach(noteEntries) { noteEntry in
          if let title = noteEntry.title,
             let content = noteEntry.content,
             let updatedAt = noteEntry.updatedAt {
            NavigationLink {
              Text(content)
            } label: {
              Text(title)
              Text(updatedAt, formatter: itemFormatter)
            }
          }
        }
      }
      .toolbar {
        ToolbarItem {
          Button(action: PersistenceController.shared.addNoteEntry) {
            Label("Add Note", systemImage: "plus")
          }
        }
      }
      Text("Select a note")
    }
  }
}

private let itemFormatter: DateFormatter = {
  let formatter = DateFormatter()
  formatter.dateStyle = .short
  formatter.timeStyle = .medium
  return formatter
}()

struct ContentView_Previews: PreviewProvider {
  static var previews: some View {
    ContentView().environment(
      \.managedObjectContext,
      PersistenceController.preview.container.viewContext)
  }
}
```

This lays out a good foundation for the next step.

✖ Run the app to verify everything is functional as before.

Adding Text Inputs

Let's add form elements to the app: an input for the title, and an input for the content.

Wait, it is not that simple! If we have 100 note entries, should there be 100 title inputs and 100 content inputs? How can we manage them in the code?

We need to modularize the code in **ContentView** even more to easily manage this. Let's make each note entry its own View!

✖ Create a new View in **ContentView.swift** called **NoteEntryView**.

ContentView.swift

```
struct NoteEntryView: View {
  var noteEntry: NoteEntry

  var body: some View {
    if let title = noteEntry.title,
       let content = noteEntry.content,
       let updatedAt = noteEntry.updatedAt {
      NavigationLink {
        Text(content)
      } label: {
        Text(title)
        Text(updatedAt, formatter: itemFormatter)
      }
    }
  }
}
```

✖ Use **NoteEntryView** in **ContentView**

ContentView.swift

```
struct ContentView: View {
  @Environment(\.managedObjectContext) private var viewContext

  @FetchRequest(
    sortDescriptors: [
      NSSortDescriptor(
        keyPath: \NoteEntry.updatedAt,
        ascending: true)
    ],
    animation: .default)
  private var noteEntries: FetchedResults<NoteEntry>

  var body: some View {
    NavigationView {
      List {
        ForEach(noteEntries) { noteEntry in
          NoteEntryView(noteEntry: noteEntry)
        }
```

```
      }
      .toolbar {
        ToolbarItem {
          Button(action: PersistenceController.shared.addNoteEntry) {
            Label("Add Note", systemImage: "plus")
          }
        }
      }
      Text("Select a note")
    }
  }
}
```

🟣 Add text inputs to **NoteEntryView**.

Update the **NoteEntryView** with the following:

ContentView.swift

```
struct NoteEntryView: View {
  var noteEntry: NoteEntry

  /// Define states to store values of the text inputs
  @State private var titleInput: String = ""
  @State private var contentInput: String = ""

  var body: some View {
    if let title = noteEntry.title,
       let content = noteEntry.content,
       let updatedAt = noteEntry.updatedAt {
      NavigationLink {
        VStack {
          /// Text field for Title. One-line Text Input.
          TextField("Title", text: $titleInput)
          /// When the view is rendered, assuming the FetchRequest is
finished
          /// update the text input with the fetched result.
          .onAppear() {
            self.titleInput = title
          }
          /// Text Editor for Content. Multi-line Text Input.
          TextEditor(text: $contentInput)
          .onAppear() {
            self.contentInput = content
          }
        }
      } label: {
        Text(title)
        Text(updatedAt, formatter: itemFormatter)
      }
    }
  }
}
```

You may notice a few changes here:

• Replace **Text()** with **TextField()** and **TextEditor()**. **Text()** displays
  plain text that users cannot update. **TextField()** and **TextEditor()** are
  inputs that users can engage with.

- Add two **@State** variables to store the values of the two inputs
- When the inputs are being displayed, i.e. **onAppear()**, assign the noteEntry information fetched from Core Date to the input values.

Now, let's run the app and verify the changes.

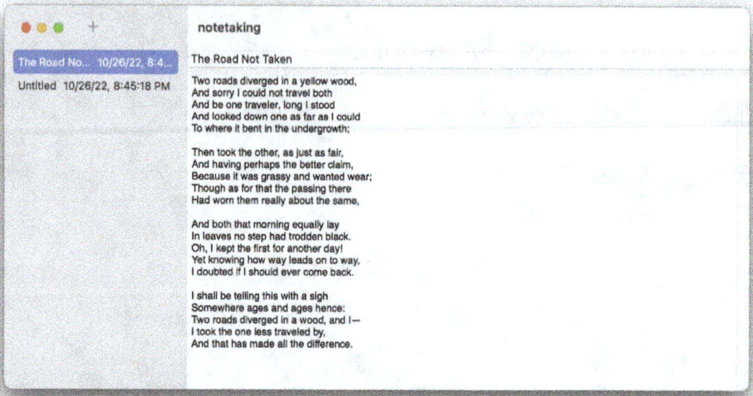

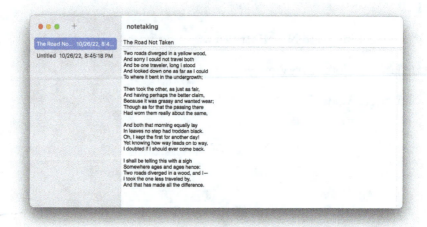

Figure 2-15 Verify the text inputs in the app

Voila! The saved note values are displayed in the inputs.

Adding Update Function

Similarly to the operations of adding note entries, we need to add a function to handle the transaction: saving the user-specified values for the title and the content to Core Data.

⌘ Add the method **updateNoteEntry()** to the **Persistence.swift**, to be next to other transactional methods such as **addNoteEntry()**.

Persistence.swift

```
func updateNoteEntry(noteEntry: NoteEntry, title:String, content: String) {
  let viewContext = container.viewContext
  noteEntry.content = content
  noteEntry.title = title
  noteEntry.updatedAt = Date()

  do {
    try viewContext.save()
  } catch {
    let nsError = error as NSError
```

```
      fatalError("Unresolved error \(nsError), \(nsError.userInfo)")
  }
}
```

Given the provided **noteEntry**, update the **content** and the **title** with the new values. Because we are updating the note entry, so we also need to update the **updatedAt** as well.

Calling Update Function When Inputs Are Changed

The input views **TextField()** and **TextEditor()** have the same method **onChange()**. This method is triggered when the input value is changed.

We need to call the update function when **onChange()** is called, so here we continue to chain **onChange()** to the inputs in the code.

✖ In **NoteEntryView**, add **onChange()** for the title input.

Title Input (ContentView.swift)

```
TextField("Title", text: $titleInput)
  .onAppear() {
    self.titleInput = title
  }
  .onChange(of: titleInput) { newTitle in
    PersistenceController.shared.updateNoteEntry(
      noteEntry: noteEntry, title: newTitle, content: contentInput)
  }
```

✖ In **NoteEntryView**, add **onChange()** for the content input.

Content Input (ContentView.swift)

```
TextEditor(text: $contentInput)
  .onAppear() {
    self.contentInput = content
  }
  .onChange(of: contentInput) { newContent in
    PersistenceController.shared.updateNoteEntry(
      noteEntry: noteEntry, title: titleInput, content: newContent)
  }
```

✖ Change the variable **noteEntry** to be **@ObservedObject**.

```
@ObservedObject var noteEntry: NoteEntry
```

This step is very important for keeping the views updated.

The variable **noteEntry** is passed from the parent **ContentView**. With the type **@ObservedObject**, whenever **noteEntry** is changed, the **NoteEntryView** will be invalidated and redrawn.

(You can also experiment by skipping this step, and see how the app behaves differently.)

With the above changes, here is what **NoteEntryView** looks like:

ContentView.swift

```swift
struct NoteEntryView: View {
  @ObservedObject var noteEntry: NoteEntry

  @State private var titleInput: String = ""
  @State private var contentInput: String = ""

  var body: some View {
    if let title = noteEntry.title,
       let updatedAt = noteEntry.updatedAt,
       let content = noteEntry.content {
      NavigationLink {
        VStack {
          TextField("Title", text: $titleInput)
            .onAppear() {
              self.titleInput = title
            }
            .onChange(of: titleInput) { newTitle in
              PersistenceController.shared.updateNoteEntry(
                noteEntry: noteEntry,
                title: newTitle,
                content: contentInput)
            }

          TextEditor(text: $contentInput)
            .onAppear() {
              self.contentInput = content
            }
            .onChange(of: contentInput) { newContent in
              PersistenceController.shared.updateNoteEntry(
                noteEntry: noteEntry,
                title: titleInput,
                content: newContent)
            }
        }
      } label: {
        Text(title)
        Text(updatedAt, formatter: itemFormatter)
      }
    }
  }
}
```

✖ Now, let's run it.

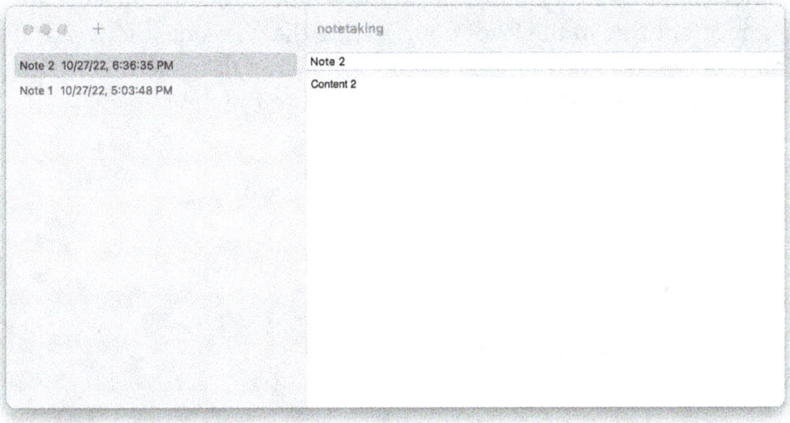

Figure 2-16 Edit the inputs, and they should be updated in Core Data

If you edit any of the inputs, you can see the updated data persists.

DELETING NOTE ENTRIES

Previously, we removed the function related to deleting. Now, let's build our version of the delete functionality.

Adding Delete Button

We will make some changes to the label of the **NoteEntryView**. This label will have a button to host the menu, which contains the button to delete a note entry.

■ Add a button to the label of **NavigationLink**.

ContentView.swift

```
HStack {
  Text(title)
  Text(updatedAt, formatter: itemFormatter)
  Spacer()
  Button {
    // TODO: add button action here
  } label: {
    Image(systemName: "minus.circle")
  }.buttonStyle(.plain)
}
```

HStack() makes all the subviews displayed horizontally. **Spacer()** plays an important role in the layout: separating the views next to it. For the views on the left side of the **Spacer()**, they align to the left. For the ones on the right side of the **Spacer()**, they align to the right.

A button shows up next to the label:

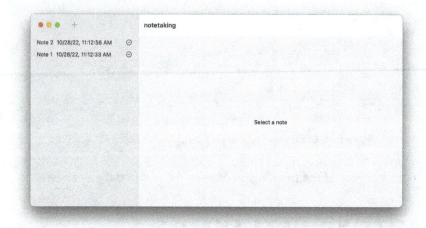

Figure 2-17 Adding a delete button on each entry

❖ Tip

Wondering how I pick the icon **minus.circle**? It is from the app SF Symbols.

SF Symbols is a library of iconography designed to integrate seamlessly with San Francisco, the system font for Apple platforms, hence the name SF.

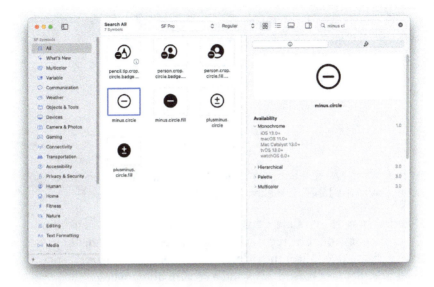

Figure 2-18 The SF Symbols app

You can simply find the icon that you need from this library, and copy the string under the icon to your code.

The app can be downloaded for free at https://developer.apple.com/sf-symbols/.

✖ Add the control to only show the delete button when hovering on the label.

We create a **@State** boolean variable **shouldShowDeleteButton** to keep the show/hide state. When the cursor hovers over the label, we set this variable to be true, otherwise, it is false. When it is true, we show the delete button, otherwise, we don't.

ContentView.swift

```swift
struct NoteEntryView: View {
    …
    @State private var shouldShowDeleteButton = false

    var body: some View {
        …
        NavigationLink {
            …
        } label: {
            HStack {
                Text(title)
                Text(updatedAt, formatter: itemFormatter)
```

```
      Spacer()
      if shouldShowDeleteButton {
        Button {
          // TODO: add button action here
        } label: {
          Image(systemName: "minus.circle")
        }.buttonStyle(.plain)
      }
    }.onHover { isHover in
      shouldShowDeleteButton = isHover
    }
  }
  }
}
```

At this point, the delete button should only show up when the cursor hovers over the label. It makes the UI cleaner.

Deletion is an irreversible transaction. Once one entry is deleted from Core Data, it cannot be recovered. A good UX design for deletion is to have a dialog to confirm the deletion intention. It avoids accidental deletions. For this reason, let's add a confirmation dialog.

✖ Add a confirmation dialog to delete a note.

ContentView.swift

```
struct NoteEntryView: View {
  …
  @State private var shouldPresentConfirm: Bool = false

  var body: some View {
    …
    NavigationLink {
      …
    } label: {
      HStack {
        Text(title)
        Text(updatedAt, formatter: itemFormatter)
        Spacer()
        if shouldShowDeleteButton || shouldPresentConfirm {
          Button {
            shouldPresentConfirm = true
          } label: {
            Image(systemName: "minus.circle")
          }.buttonStyle(.plain)
            .confirmationDialog("Are you sure?",
                                isPresented: $shouldPresentConfirm) {
              Button("Delete this note", role: .destructive) {
                // call the delete function here
              }
            }
        }
      }
    }.onHover { isHover in
      shouldShowDeleteButton = isHover
    }
  }
  }
}
```

In this change, we create a new **@State** variable **shouldPresentConfirm** to control the show/hide of the confirmation dialog.

We also chain a **confirmationDialog()** to the delete button.

The benefits of a confirmation dialog are:

- No need to add a cancel button. The confirmation dialog includes a standard dismiss action by default.

- All actions in the confirmation dialog dismiss the dialog. You don't need to handle the actions separately.

Adding Delete Function

Deleting a note is also transactional, so it can be placed into **PersistenceController** in **Persistence.swift**.

✖ Add a function **deleteNoteEntry** in **PersistenceController**

Persistence.swift

```
func deleteNoteEntry(noteEntry: NoteEntry) {
  let viewContext = container.viewContext
  viewContext.delete(noteEntry)
  do {
    try viewContext.save()
  } catch {
    let nsError = error as NSError
    fatalError("Unresolved error \(nsError), \(nsError.userInfo)")
  }
}
```

Wiring Delete Button with Delete Function

The last step is to connect the dots between the function and the UI.

✖ Call the **deleteNoteEntry** inside delete button.

ContentView.swift

```
Button {
  shouldPresentConfirm = true
} label: {
  Image(systemName: "minus.circle")
}.buttonStyle(.plain)
  .confirmationDialog("Are you sure?",
                      isPresented: $shouldPresentConfirm) {
    Button("Delete this note", role: .destructive) {
      PersistenceController.shared.deleteNoteEntry(noteEntry: noteEntry)
    }
  }
```

- Run the app. Now you should be able to delete a note by clicking the delete button and confirming.

Fantastic! The basic functionality of a note-taking app is complete.

CLEAN-UP

Removing the Entity Item

As we are not using the entity Item anymore, it is okay to remove the entity.

- Simply click to select the entity Item, and hit the **delete** key on the keyboard.

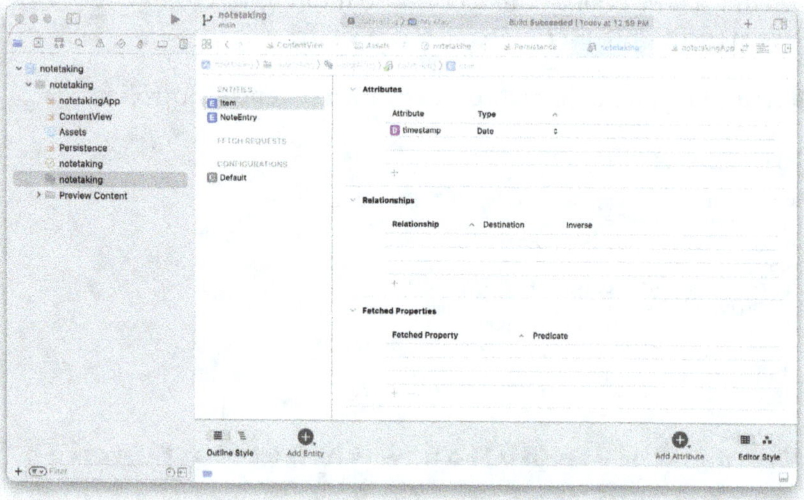

Figure 2-19 Select the entity Item, and hit delete

Once the entity is deleted, broken code may rise when you attempt to run the app, like the following:

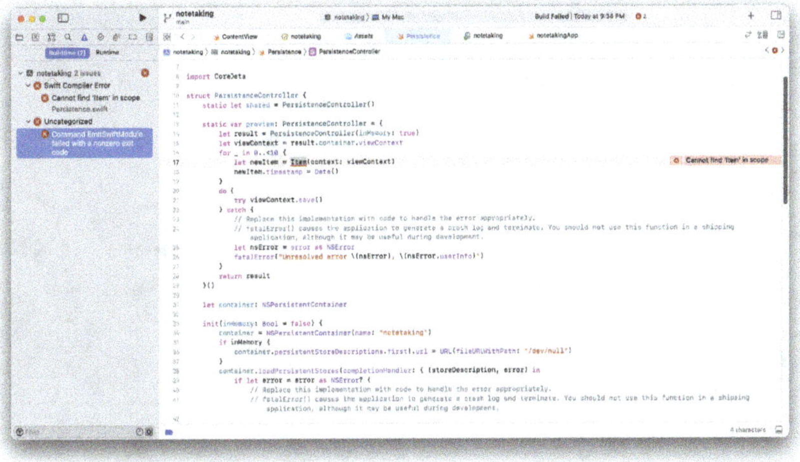

Figure 2-20 Errors rise after the entity Item is deleted

Use the error messages as hints to fix the issues.

In this case, **PersistenceContainer** is responsible to set up the **Item** mock data for the preview in canvas. Previously, it set up a set of 10 items. Here, we can similarly reuse and modify it for **NoteEntry**.

⌘ Update the for loop to the following:

Persistence.swift

```
for _ in 0..<10 {
  let newNoteEntry = NoteEntry(context: viewContext)
  newNoteEntry.createdAt = Date()
  newNoteEntry.updatedAt = Date()
  newNoteEntry.content = "(Content)"
  newNoteEntry.title = "(title)"
}
```

⌘ Go to **ContentView.swift**, and hit **Option-Command-P**. It should update the **Preview** window. The mock data should be reflected in Figure 2-21.

Figure 2-21 Preview with mock data

✖️ Run the app. The errors should disappear. The app should be built successfully.

DRY (Don't Repeat Yourself)

One of the engineering principles is Don't Repeat Yourself, short for DRY. It means reducing the code repetition.

As we've created multiple methods in **PersistenceContainer** to manage the transactions in Core Data, you can easily see some code repetition.

Persistence.swift

```
import CoreData

struct PersistenceController {
  static let shared = PersistenceController()
  ...
  func addNoteEntry() {
    let viewContext = container.viewContext
    let newNoteEntry = NoteEntry(context: viewContext)
    newNoteEntry.createdAt = Date()
    newNoteEntry.updatedAt = Date()
    newNoteEntry.title = "Untitled"
    newNoteEntry.content = "TBD"

    do {
      try viewContext.save()
    } catch {
      let nsError = error as NSError
      fatalError("Unresolved error \(nsError), \(nsError.userInfo)")
    }
  }
}
```

```swift
func updateNoteEntry(
    noteEntry: NoteEntry, title:String, content: String) {
    let viewContext = container.viewContext
    noteEntry.content = content
    noteEntry.title = title
    noteEntry.updatedAt = Date()

    do {
      try viewContext.save()
    } catch {
      let nsError = error as NSError
      fatalError("Unresolved error \(nsError), \(nsError.userInfo)")
    }
  }

  func deleteNoteEntry(noteEntry: NoteEntry) {
    let viewContext = container.viewContext
    viewContext.delete(noteEntry)
    do {
      try viewContext.save()
    } catch {
      let nsError = error as NSError
      fatalError("Unresolved error \(nsError), \(nsError.userInfo)")
    }
  }
}
```

✖ Create a private function for saving **viewContext**.

Extract the common part out to its own function, and it looks this:

Persistence.swift

```swift
func save() {
  let viewContext = container.viewContext
  do {
    try viewContext.save()
  } catch {
    let nsError = error as NSError
    fatalError("Unresolved error \(nsError), \(nsError.userInfo)")
  }
}
```

✖ Update the caller functions to call **save()**.

Persistence.swift

```swift
func addNoteEntry() {
  let newNoteEntry = NoteEntry(context: container.viewContext)
  newNoteEntry.createdAt = Date()
  newNoteEntry.updatedAt = Date()
  newNoteEntry.title = "Untitled"
  newNoteEntry.content = "TBD"

  save()
}

func updateNoteEntry(noteEntry: NoteEntry, title:String, content: String) {
  noteEntry.content = content
  noteEntry.title = title
  noteEntry.updatedAt = Date()
```

```
    save()
}

func deleteNoteEntry(noteEntry: NoteEntry) {
  container.viewContext.delete(noteEntry)
  save()
}
```

✖ Run the app to confirm it is working.

As you add more features to the app, there will be more scenarios like this. Refactor like this as you see fit.

FULL CODE

Hope you have been following along so far.

If not, don't worry! I got you covered. You can always check out the entire codebase of this project.

You can find the code on Github: https://github.com/higracehuang/macos-app-notetaking

CHAPTER 3: BUILDING A WINDOWLESS SCREENSHOT APP

Now, with the experience of building the note-taking app, you've already learned a lot about macOS apps and SwiftUI.

Let's do something different to learn other aspects of macOS development: creating a menu bar, and interfacing with other apps in the OS.

This is the app that we are going to build:

Figure 3-1 What the app looks like in the end

By building this app, we will get familiar with:

- Usage of Status Bar

- Windowless app

- How to interact with native apps on macOS

- Basics of SwiftUI

REQUIREMENTS FOR THIS APP

This app needs to have the following features:

- A user can access the functionality via the status bar
- A user can screenshot by selecting an area on the screen, a window, or capturing the entire screen
- No main window needed

CREATING A MACOS APP

■ Create a macOS project named **EasyScreenshot**. Note that, **Use Core Data** is unchecked. We don't need Core Data in this project.

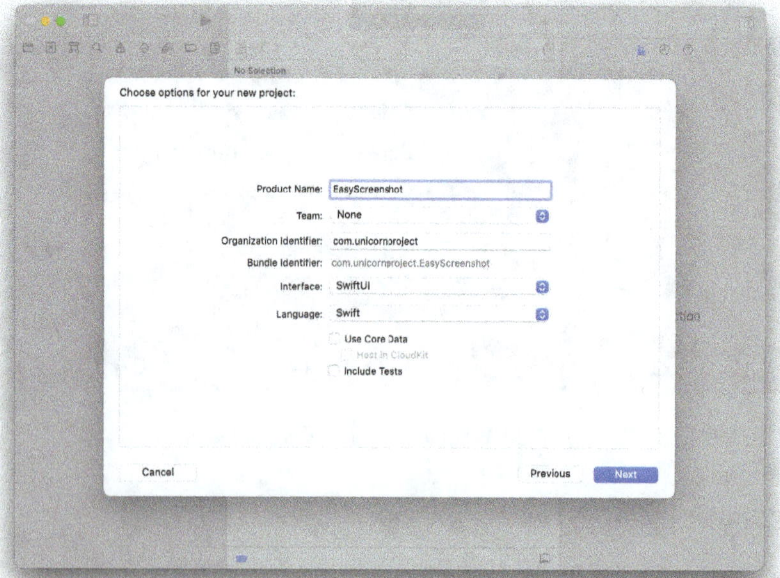

Figure 3-2 Filling the project information: keeping Use Core Data unchecked

■ Check the starter project. It is pretty simple.

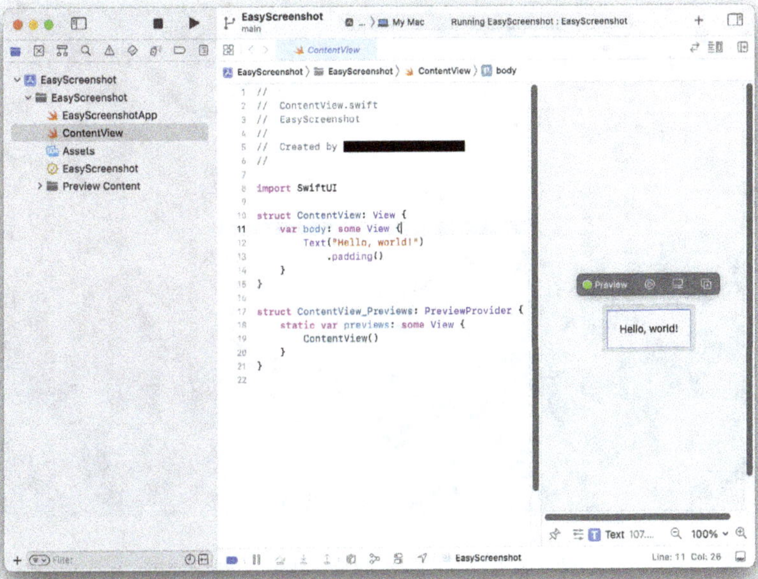

Figure 3-3 The default code after the project is created

- Run the app. The starter app looks like the following:

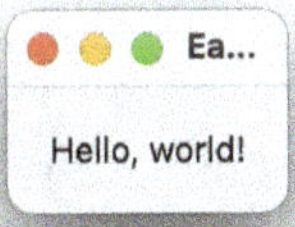

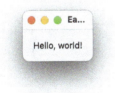

Figure 3-4 What the app looks like when the project is just created.

CREATING A STATUS BAR ICON

Figure 3-5 What a status bar icon looks like

✖ Create a new file called **AppDelegate.swift**. Within the new file, set it to show a status item in the menu bar.

In this file, we create a delegate object for the application. What does it mean? It means, when the application reaches a certain state, the Application Delegate will receive notifications.

The most important states are:

- **applicationDidFinishLaunching**: it is great for startup configuration and construction.

- **applicationWillTerminate**: it is great for clean-up after the app ends

In this app, we want to set up a menu in the status bar at the startup time, so **applicationDidFinishLaunching** is perfect for this case.

The full code of **AppDelegate.swift** is the following:

AppDelegate.swift

```swift
import SwiftUI

class AppDelegate: NSObject, NSApplicationDelegate {
  var statusBarItem: NSStatusItem?
  func applicationDidFinishLaunching(_ notification: Notification) {
```

```
    statusBarItem = NSStatusBar.system
      .statusItem(withLength: NSStatusItem.squareLength)
    if let statusBarButton = statusBarItem?.button {
      statusBarButton.image = NSImage(
        systemSymbolName: "cursorarrow.rays",
        accessibilityDescription: nil
      )
    }

    let mainMenu = NSMenu()

    statusBarItem?.menu = mainMenu
  }
}
```

✖ Instantiate **AppDelegate** in **EasyScreenShotApp.swift**.

EasyScreenshotApp.swift

```
import SwiftUI

@main
struct EasyScreenshotApp: App {
  @NSApplicationDelegateAdaptor(AppDelegate.self)
  private var appDelegate

  var body: some Scene {
    WindowGroup {
      ContentView()
    }
  }
}
```

✖ Run the app. You should see an icon like this on the status bar. At this moment, it should do nothing yet when you click on it.

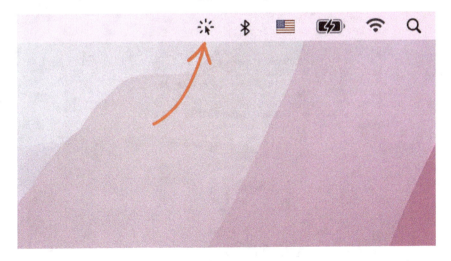

Figure 3-6 The status bar icon

❖ Tip

From macOS 13.0 (Ventura, released on October 2022), you can use MenuBarExtra to easily create such a menu in the status bar instead of using Application Delegate.

However, in this book, we continue to use Application Delegate, as it is compatible with older OS versions.

✖ Create a Menu with multiple menu items

Create an object of **NSMenu**, and also create several **NSMenuItem** objects. In each **NSMenuItem** object, define the name of the item, the icon, and the action.

AppDelegate.swift

```swift
import SwiftUI

class AppDelegate: NSObject, NSApplicationDelegate {
  var statusBarItem: NSStatusItem?
  func applicationDidFinishLaunching(_ notification: Notification) {

    statusBarItem = NSStatusBar.system
      .statusItem(withLength: NSStatusItem.squareLength)
    if let statusBarButton = statusBarItem?.button {
      statusBarButton.image = NSImage(
        systemSymbolName: "cursorarrow.rays",
        accessibilityDescription: nil
      )
    }

    let mainMenu = NSMenu()

    /// Creating menu item: area capture
    let itemSelectArea = NSMenuItem(
      title: "Select an area",
      action: #selector(Self.actionSelectArea(_:)),
      keyEquivalent: "")
    itemSelectArea.image = NSImage(
      systemSymbolName: "rectangle.dashed",
      accessibilityDescription: nil
    )
    itemSelectArea.target = self
    mainMenu.addItem(itemSelectArea)

    /// Creating menu item: entire screen capture
    let itemCaptureEntireScreen = NSMenuItem(
      title: "Screenshot the entire screen",
      action: #selector(Self.actionCaptureEntireScreen(_:)),
      keyEquivalent: "")
    itemCaptureEntireScreen.image = NSImage(
      systemSymbolName: "macwindow.on.rectangle",
      accessibilityDescription: nil
    )
    itemCaptureEntireScreen.target = self
    mainMenu.addItem(itemCaptureEntireScreen)

    /// Creating menu item: window capture
```

```swift
    let itemCaptureWindow = NSMenuItem(
      title: "Capture a window",
      action: #selector(self.actionCaptureWindow(_:)),
      keyEquivalent: "")
    itemCaptureWindow.image = NSImage(
      systemSymbolName: "macwindow",
      accessibilityDescription: nil
    )
    itemCaptureWindow.target = self
    mainMenu.addItem(itemCaptureWindow)

    /// Creating a divider
    mainMenu.addItem(.separator())

    /// Creating menu item:  quit the app
    let itemQuit = NSMenuItem(
      title: "Quit EasyScreenshot",
      action: #selector(self.actionExitApp(_:)),
      keyEquivalent: "")
    itemQuit.target = self
    mainMenu.addItem(itemQuit)

    statusBarItem?.menu = mainMenu
  }

  @objc private func actionExitApp(_ sender: Any?) {
    NSApp.terminate(self)
  }

  @objc private func actionCaptureEntireScreen(_ sender: Any?) {

  }

  @objc private func actionSelectArea(_ sender: Any?) {

  }

  @objc private func actionCaptureWindow(_ sender: Any?) {

  }
}
```

❖ Tip

You may have noticed the class with the prefix NS, and wondered what
it means. **NS** comes from **NextSTEP**, the original operating system that
became Mac OS X when Apple acquired Next.

> *Historical Note: If you're wondering why so many of the classes you
> encounter have an NS prefix, it's because of the past history of Cocoa and
> Cocoa Touch. Cocoa began life as the collected frameworks used to build
> apps for the NeXTStep operating system. When Apple purchased NeXT
> back in 1996, much of NeXTStep was incorporated into OS X, including
> the existing class names. Cocoa Touch was introduced as the iOS
> equivalent of Cocoa; some classes are available in both Cocoa and Cocoa
> Touch, though there are also a large number of classes unique to each*

platform. Two-letter prefixes like NS and UI (for User Interface elements on iOS) are reserved for use by Apple.[3]

✖ Run the app. When you click on the icon, it should show a menu like Figure 3-7.

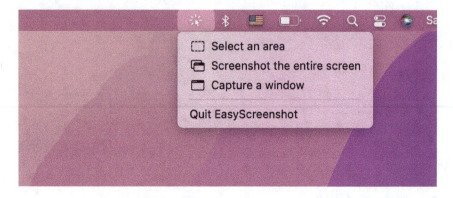

Figure 3-7 The Menu in the status bar

REMOVE THE MAIN WINDOW

You may also see a window still show up. However, we don't need it for this app.

It requires a file called **Info.plist** to declare your app's use of encryption. However, this file is not created by default.

✖ In order to create the Info.plist, go to **File** > **New** > **File...** > Choose **Property List** under **Resource** > Click **Next** -> Save As **Info** > Click **Create**. If you already have a .plist file, you can skip this step.

---

[3] https://developer.apple.com/library/archive/documentation/Cocoa/ Conceptual/ProgrammingWithObjectiveC/DefiningClasses/ DefiningClasses.html

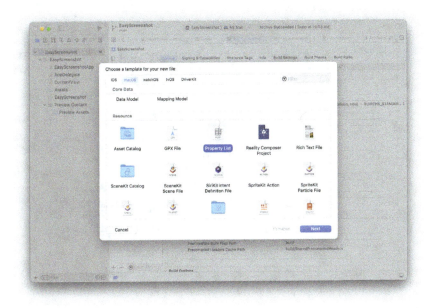

Figure 3-8 Creating a Property List file

✖ Link the newly created Info.plist, by going to **Build Settings ->**
Search **Info.plist** > Fill the path with **Info.plist**.

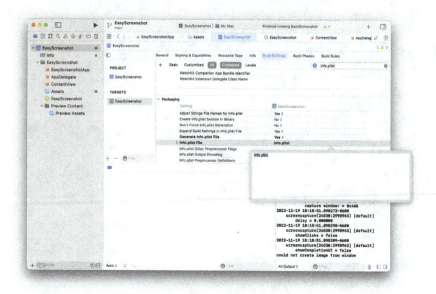

Figure 3-9 Linking the Info.plist

�֎ Click on the **Info.plist** > right click **Information Property List** > type A**pplication is agent(UIElement), Boolean, Yes.**

What does **Application is agent(UIElement)** mean? It indicates the app is an agent app that runs in the background and doesn't appear in the dock. It is one of the key things needed to get rid of the window.

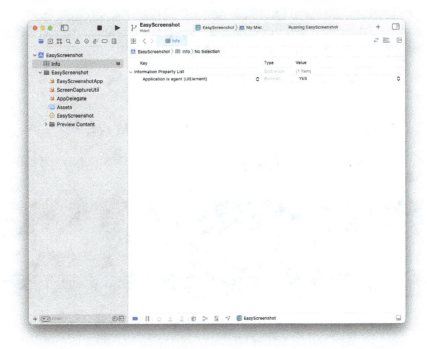

Figure 3-10 Info.plist

✖ Update the Scene of the App: replacing it with **Settings()** and **EmptyView()**.

EasyScreenshotApp.swift

```swift
import SwiftUI

@main
struct EasyScreenshotApp: App {
  @NSApplicationDelegateAdaptor(AppDelegate.self)
  private var appDelegate

  var body: some Scene {
    Settings {
      EmptyView()
    }
  }
}
```

✖ Run the app, to confirm that the main window is not showing up anymore, but the menu in the status bar stays.

At this point, we should have the desired user interface for this app, however, the functionalities do not exist yet. For example, if you click on any item on the menu, nothing happens.

In the next few sections, let's fill in the functionalities.

THE SCREENSHOT APP ON MAC

The screenshot functionality already exists On macOS. It is an app called **Screenshot**.

Figure 3-11 The Screenshot App on macOS

You can use this to screenshot the full screen, the selected window, or a selected area.

We will take advantage of this native app.

Run CLI of the Screenshot App

Now, we need to figure out how to call the **Screenshot** app from the Terminal:

```
screencapture -h
```

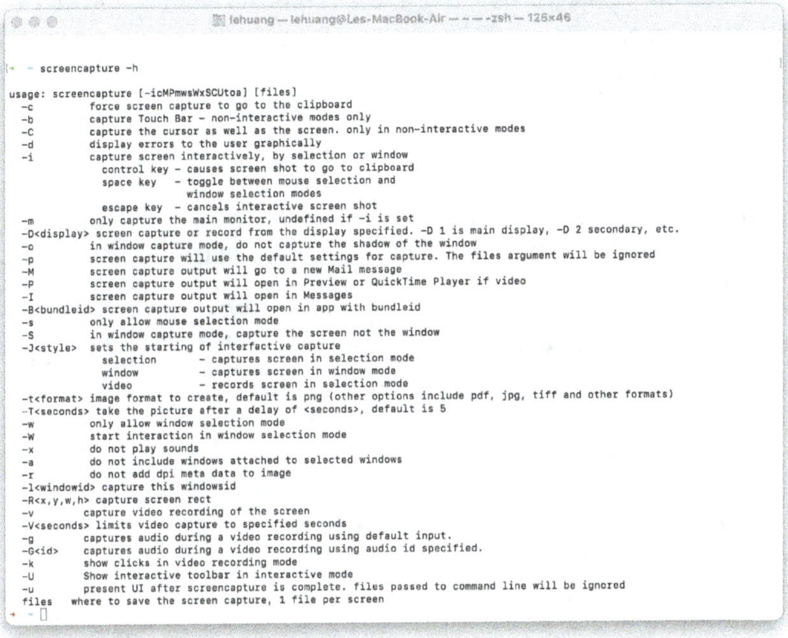

```
lehuang — lehuang@Les-MacBook-Air — ~ — -zsh — 125x46

|+ - screencapture -h

usage: screencapture [-icMPmwsWxSCUtoa] [files]
  -c             force screen capture to go to the clipboard
  -b             capture Touch Bar - non-interactive modes only
  -C             capture the cursor as well as the screen. only in non-interactive modes
  -d             display errors to the user graphically
  -i             capture screen interactively, by selection or window
                   control key - causes screen shot to go to clipboard
                   space key   - toggle between mouse selection and
                                 window selection modes
                   escape key  - cancels interactive screen shot
  -m             only capture the main monitor, undefined if -i is set
  -D<display>    screen capture or record from the display specified. -D 1 is main display, -D 2 secondary, etc.
  -o             in window capture mode, do not capture the shadow of the window
  -p             screen capture will use the default settings for capture. The files argument will be ignored
  -M             screen capture output will go to a new Mail message
  -P             screen capture output will open in Preview or QuickTime Player if video
  -I             screen capture output will open in Messages
  -B<bundleid>   screen capture output will open in app with bundleid
  -s             only allow mouse selection mode
  -S             in window capture mode, capture the screen not the window
  -J<style>      sets the starting of interactive capture
                   selection        - captures screen in selection mode
                   window           - captures screen in window mode
                   video            - records screen in selection mode
  -t<format>  image format to create, default is png (other options include pdf, jpg, tiff and other formats)
  -T<seconds> take the picture after a delay of <seconds>, default is 5
  -w             only allow window selection mode
  -W             start interaction in window selection mode
  -x             do not play sounds
  -a             do not include windows attached to selected windows
  -r             do not add dpi meta data to image
  -l<windowid> capture this windowsid
  -R<x,y,w,h> capture screen rect
  -v             capture video recording of the screen
  -V<seconds> limits video capture to specified seconds
  -g             captures audio during a video recording using default input.
  -G<id>         captures audio during a video recording using audio id specified.
  -k             show clicks in video recording mode
  -U             Show interactive toolbar in interactive mode
  -u             present UI after screencapture is complete. files passed to command line will be ignored
  files       where to save the screen capture, 1 file per screen
+ - []
```

Figure 3-12 The instructions of screencapture

Our requirement is to capture the screen via the following ways and store them in the clipboard.

1. user selected area

2. window selection

3. fullscreen

The corresponding commands will be:

```
1. screencapture -cs
2. screencapture -cw
3. screencapture -cm
```

You can try the commands above and see how they behave.

CALL SCREENSHOT FROM APP

Now, let's call these commands from the **EasyScreenshot** app.

The following snippet is how to call the command **screencapture** from an external app:

```swift
let task = Process()
task.launchPath = "/usr/sbin/screencapture"
task.arguments = ["-cw"]
task.launch()
task.waitUntilExit()
```

✖ Create a utility class to handle screen capture-related actions: create a new file called **ScreenCaptureUtil.swift**, and update the class with the following.

ScreenCaptureUtil.swift

```swift
import SwiftUI

enum ScreenshotType {
  case EntireScreen
  case Window
  case UserSelection
}

class ScreenCaptureUtil {

  static func screenshot(type: ScreenshotType) {
    let task = Process()
    task.launchPath = "/usr/sbin/screencapture"

    switch type {
    case .EntireScreen:
      task.arguments = ["-cm"]
    case .Window:
      task.arguments = ["-cw"]
    case .UserSelection:
      task.arguments = ["-cs"]
    }

    task.launch()
    task.waitUntilExit()
  }
}
```

We create a new enum to differentiate the 3 types of screenshots. When the **screenshot()** is being called, the enum variable will tell which screenshot type is.

✖ Call the **screenshot()** when the menu item is clicked.

AppDelegate.swift

```swift
@objc private func actionCaptureEntireScreen(_ sender: Any?) {
  ScreenCaptureUtil.screenshot(type: .EntireScreen)
}

@objc private func actionSelectArea(_ sender: Any?) {
  ScreenCaptureUtil.screenshot(type: .UserSelection)
}

@objc private func actionCaptureWindow(_ sender: Any?) {
```

```
    ScreenCaptureUtil.screenshot(type: .Window)
}
```

✖ Run the app, and try it out.

Figure 3-13 The dropdown menu

✖ Click on one of the options in the menu. It may do nothing. Check
  the **Output** window, you can see the following.

```
2022-11-06 22:00:46.885250-0600 screencapture[55227:3571989] [default]
launched with commandline
2022-11-06 22:00:46.900863-0600 screencapture[55227:3571989] [] Unable to
access preferences for Siri Learning toggles. Disabling checks.
2022-11-06 22:00:46.901606-0600 screencapture[55227:3571992] [] XPC error:
Error Domain=NSCocoaErrorDomain Code=4099 "The connection to service named
com.apple.coreduetd.knowledge.user was invalidated: failed at lookup with
error 159 - Sandbox restriction." UserInfo={NSDebugDescription=The
connection to service named com.apple.coreduetd.knowledge.user was
invalidated: failed at lookup with error 159 - Sandbox restriction.}
2022-11-06 22:00:46.901726-0600 screencapture[55227:3571991] [BiomeSource]
Error persisting discoverability signal event to knowledge store Error
Domain=NSCocoaErrorDomain Code=4099 "The connection to service named
com.apple.coreduetd.knowledge.user was invalidated: failed at lookup with
error 159 - Sandbox restriction." UserInfo={NSDebugDescription=The
connection to service named com.apple.coreduetd.knowledge.user was
invalidated: failed at lookup with error 159 - Sandbox restriction.}
2022-11-06 22:00:46.909382-0600 screencapture[55227:3571989] [0x44c:
Permission denied]
screencapture: cannot run two interactive screen captures at a time
```

To solve this, we need to update the **Entitlements** file. This file stores
the configuration for different capabilities of an app. In our case, we
need to declare the app's screenshot ability.

Where can we find the **Entitlements** file? It is in the project directory,
named **EasyScreenshot.entitlements**.

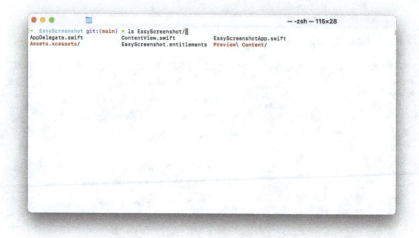

Figure 3-14 *The entitlement file in the directory of the project EasyScreenshot*

To fix this, we will need to update the entitlements file by adding the attribute. Remember to clean the build folder, and build again.

EasyScreenshot.entitlements

```
<key>com.apple.security.temporary-exception.mach-register.global-name</key>
<string>com.apple.screencapture.interactive</string>
```

The entitlements file will look at this:

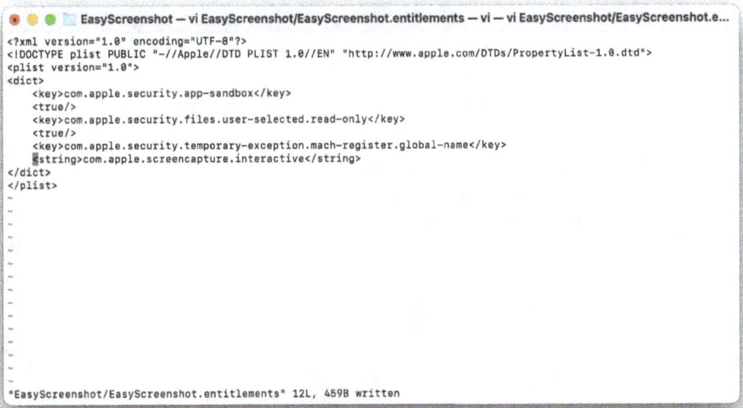

Figure 3-15 What the entitlements file look like

❖ Tip

What are entitlements? An entitlement is a right or privilege that grants an executable particular capabilities, such as iCloud storage, push notifications, Apple Pay, and App Sandbox. An app stores entitlements as key-value pairs embedded in the code signature of its binary executable.

❋ Run the app again. The error should be gone.

❋ Click on one of the options in the menu. You should see a dialog like below: to ask you to grant permission to record the computer screen.

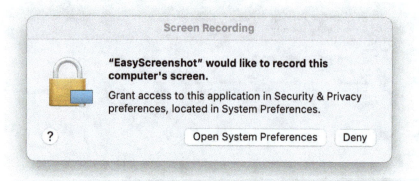

Figure 3-16 The permission dialog for using Screen Recording

❖ Click **Open System Preferences**. You should see a dialog of **Security & Privacy**, and the checkbox of **EasyScreenshot** is turned off (Figure 3-17).

Figure 3-17 The Security & Privacy dialog before turning on the permission for EasyScreenshot

Figure 3-18 The Security & Privacy dialog after turning on the permission for EasyScreenshot

✖ Grant the screen recording permission for **EasyScreenshot** (Figure 3-18). It may ask you to restart the app.

✖ Once the app is restarted, click one of the options, and it should start to do screenshots. You can see the captured image by pasting it into any editor, for example, Google Docs, or Microsoft Word.

Pretty cool, right? Now you can easily get access to the screenshot functionalities via the status bar!

FULL CODE

I hope the steps are easy to follow. if you get lost during the process, don't worry. You can always check out the full code of the project.

The full code can be accessed at https://github.com/higracehuang/EasyScreenshot.

CHAPTER 4: BUILDING A PHOTO FETCHING APP

The two apps we built earlier are local. They don't handle network connections. Many real-world use cases require data transmission with backend services. For example, a macOS client for the Twitter app that fetches the latest tweets for a user, or a weather app that needs to pull forecasts for different locations.

In this chapter, let's build a simple photo app that interacts with HTTP requests.

By building this app, we will get familiar with

- Fetching HTTP requests

- Basics of SwiftUI, including ScrollView, AsyncImage

REQUIREMENTS FOR THIS APP

This app needs to have the following features:

- A user can fetch photos from a remote server

- A user can see browser all the photos

- When a photo is clicked, a user can visit the original website

CREATING A MACOS APP

✚ Create a macOS project named **SimplePhotos**. Note that, **Use Core Data** is unchecked. We don't need Core Data in this project.

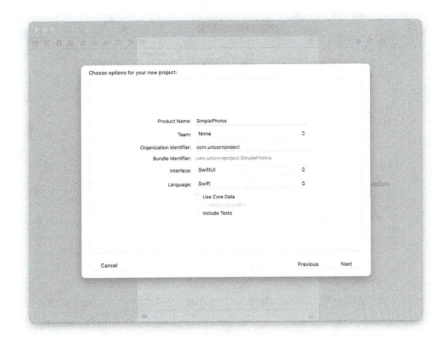

Figure 4-1 Create a new project

PREPARING NETWORK CALLS TO FETCH PHOTOS

Before creating any user interface, we can start ready for the network API calls. Once it is done, we can wire it up with the user interface.

To simplify this tutorial, in this project, we use an existing service provided by JSONPlaceholder[4]. But for your future projects, you may need to set up your servers.

Here is a sample of the JSON returned from https://jsonplaceholder.typicode.com/photos:

```
[
  {
    "albumId": 1,
    "id": 1,
    "title": "accusamus beatae ad facilis cum similique qui sunt",
    "url": "https://via.placeholder.com/600/92c952",
```

---

[4] https://jsonplaceholder.typicode.com

```
    "thumbnailUrl": "https://via.placeholder.com/150/92c952"
  },
  {
    "albumId": 1,
    "id": 2,
    "title": "reprehenderit est deserunt velit ipsam",
    "url": "https://via.placeholder.com/600/771796",
    "thumbnailUrl": "https://via.placeholder.com/150/771796"
  },
  {
    "albumId": 1,
    "id": 3,
    "title": "officia porro iure quia iusto qui ipsa ut modi",
    "url": "https://via.placeholder.com/600/24f355",
    "thumbnailUrl": "https://via.placeholder.com/150/24f355"
  },
  {
    "albumId": 1,
    "id": 4,
    "title": "culpa odio esse rerum omnis laboriosam voluptate repudiandae",
    "url": "https://via.placeholder.com/600/d32776",
    "thumbnailUrl": "https://via.placeholder.com/150/d32776"
  },
  …
]
```

It is an array of objects. An object contains all the information about a photo.

� Create the data model for the API response.

Create a new Swift file called **Photo.swift**. This stores the data for one photo. The goal is to map the JSON response to a data structure in Swift, which will be easily used in the code.

Photo.swift

```swift
import Foundation

struct Photo: Codable, Hashable {
  let albumId: Int
  let id: Int
  let title: String
  let url: String
  let thumbnailUrl: String
}
```

So you can see, the keys in this struct match the keys in the JSON.

✘ Create a method to fetch JSON for photos.

Create a new Swift file called ApiCall.

ApiCall.swift

```swift
import Foundation

class ApiCall {
  static func getPhotos(completion:@escaping ([Photo]) -> ()) {
```

```
    let getPhotosUrlString = "https://jsonplaceholder.typicode.com/photos"
    guard let url = URL(string: getPhotosUrlString) else { return }

    URLSession.shared.dataTask(with: url) { (data, response, error) in

      if let data = data {
        if let photos = try?
            JSONDecoder().decode([Photo].self, from: data) {
          DispatchQueue.main.async {
            completion(photos)
          }
          return
        }
      }
      print(
        "Fetch failed: \(error?.localizedDescription ?? "Unknown error")")
    }.resume()
  }
}
```

In this method **getPhotos()**, **URLSession** is used to make a network call to fetch the Photos. When the response returns, **JSONDecoder()** is used to parse the response that matches the array of **Photo**.

URLSession works in a background thread, although it does not specifically show. So the network call to fetch photos is on a background thread, not the main thread where UI work happens.

Important to note that, it is okay to parse the JSON on a background thread, but it is a no-no to do any user interface work there.

Here, we are on a background thread processing JSON. When it is complete and the UI needs to be updated with parsed data, it should return to the main thread, by calling **DispatchQueue.main.async()**.

⌘ Turn on **Ongoing Connections (Client)**.

By default, a macOS app cannot make network calls. It is to protect system resources and user data. To enable the network connections, we need to request it through entitlements.

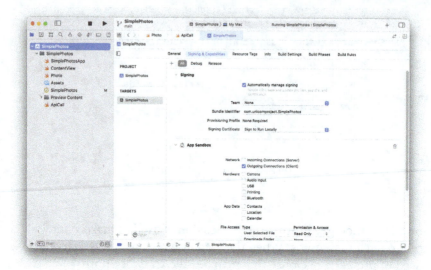

Figure 4-2 Turn on Ongoing Connections

Go to **SimplePhotos(Project)** > **SimplePhotos(Target)** > **Signing & Capabilities** > **Under App Sandbox -> Turn on Ongoing Connections (Client)**, as shown in Figure 4-2.

The configuration above will modify the file **SimplePhotos.entitlements**.

This step is very important. If skipped, no network calls will be made. (You can try it by skipping this step and moving on to the next steps, so you can see the difference.)

CREATING USER INTERFACE

By this point, you cannot see any difference rather than a blank app. In this section, we will add the user interface.

In the app, we can have a **PhotoView** to manage individual photos and a **ScrollView** to house them, as shown in Figure 4-3

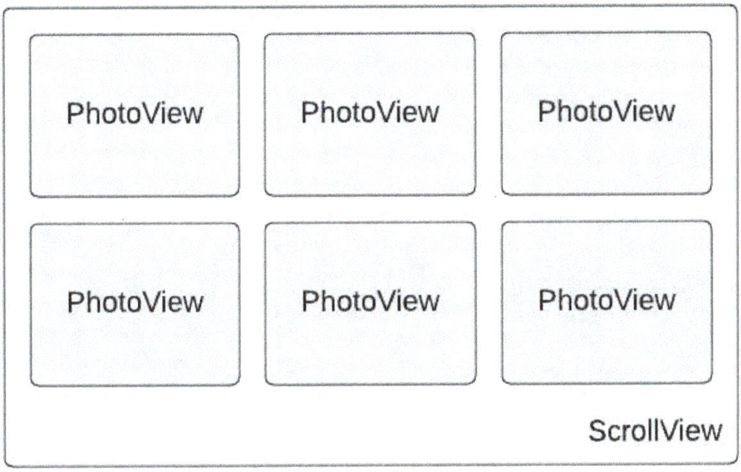

Figure 4-3 A ScrollView with a collection of PhotoViews

■ Create a SwiftUI View called **PhotoView.**

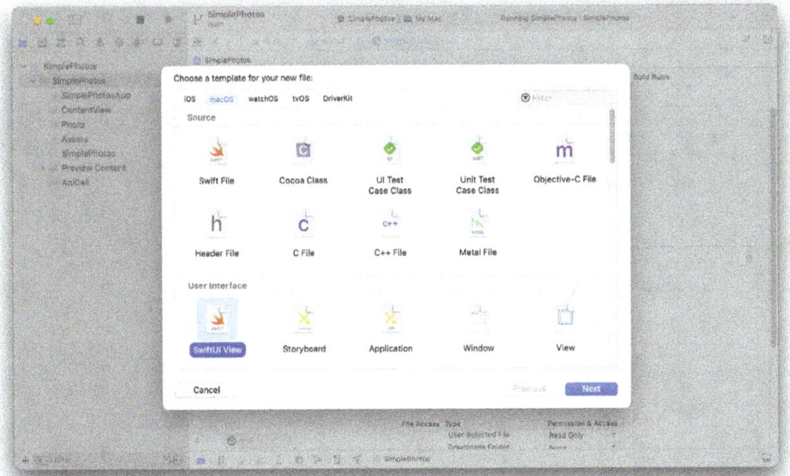

Figure 4-4 Create a new SwiftUi View

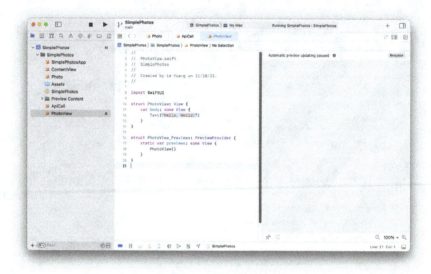

Figure 4-5 The code generated by SwiftUI view creation for PhotoView

✖ Layout a basic view structure for **PhotoView.**

PhotoView.swift

```swift
import SwiftUI

struct PhotoView: View {
  var photoData: Photo

  var body: some View {
    ZStack(alignment: .bottom) {
      AsyncImage(url: URL(string: photoData.thumbnailUrl)) { image in
        image
          .resizable()
          .aspectRatio(contentMode: .fill)
      } placeholder: {
        Color.gray
      }.frame(width: 200, height: 200)

      Text(photoData.title)
        .padding(5)
        .foregroundColor(.black)
        .frame(width: 200)
        .lineLimit(2)
    }
  }
}

struct PhotoView_Previews_Long: PreviewProvider {
  static var previews: some View {
    PhotoView(photoData: Photo(
      albumId: 1,
      id: 1,
      title: "short",
      url: "https://via.placeholder.com/600/92c952",
      thumbnailUrl: "https://via.placeholder.com/200/92c952"))
```

```
    }
}
struct PhotoView_Previews_Short: PreviewProvider {
  static var previews: some View {
    PhotoView(photoData: Photo(
      albumId: 1,
      id: 1,
      title: "officia delectus consequatur vero aut veniam",
      url: "https://via.placeholder.com/160/56a8c2",
      thumbnailUrl: "https://via.placeholder.com/150/56a8c2"))
  }
}
```

From the code above, you may notice a few things:

- The PhotoView is wrapped with **ZStack** with **AsyncImage** in the back and Text in the front.

- **AsyncImage()** is used to display an image fetched by a network call.

- The fetched image is resized to fill the frame of 200 x 200.

- When the image is not received, it shows a placeholder with a gray background.

- The title of the photo is displayed in black with a limit of 2 lines.

- Two previews are added, so we can compare how the view looks with different lengths of content.

We can see the preview of **PhotoView** via **Option-Command-P**:

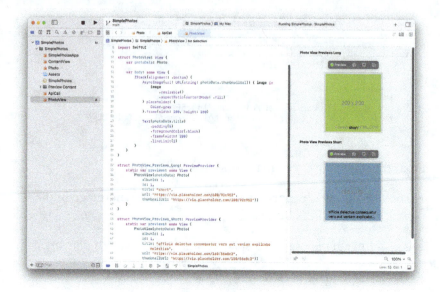

Figure 4-6 Preview of PhotoView on the right pane

✖ In **ContentView.swift**, create a **ScrollView** to contain all
   PhotoViews.

ContentView.swift

```swift
import SwiftUI

struct ContentView: View {
  @State var photos:[Photo] = []

  let columns = [GridItem](repeating: GridItem(.flexible()), count: 4)

  var body: some View {
    ScrollView {
      LazyVGrid(columns: columns) {
        ForEach(photos, id: \.self) { photo in
          PhotoView(photoData: photo)
        }
      }
      .padding(.horizontal)
      .onAppear {
        ApiCall.getPhotos(completion: { photos in
          self.photos = photos
        })
      }.padding()
    }.frame(minWidth: 900, minHeight: 800)
  }
}

struct ContentView_Previews: PreviewProvider {
  static var previews: some View {
    ContentView()
  }
}
```

From the code above, you may notice a few things:

- Introduce a **@State** variable called photos to store the result of the **ApiCall.getPhotos()**.

- Define **ScrollView** with a 4-column **LazyVGrid**.

- Inside the **LazyVGrid**, display all the **PhotoView**s.

- When the view appears, make a call to **ApiCall.getPhotos()** to fetch all photos, implicitly in the background thread.

- The overall size of the app window is 900 x 800.

❖ Tip

LazyVGrid is a container view that arranges its child views in a grid that grows vertically, creating items only when they need to be displayed. On the contrary, a **Grid** view creates its child views right away.

A "sister" of **LazyVGrid** is **LazyHGrid**. **LazyHGrid** arranges its child views in a grid that grows horizontally.

❖ Tip

ScrollView is a scrollable container view where you can display content. This view automatically adjusts its size to fit the content inside. **ScrollView** can be scrolled horizontally, vertically, or both.

We can see the preview of PhotoView via **Option-Command-P**:

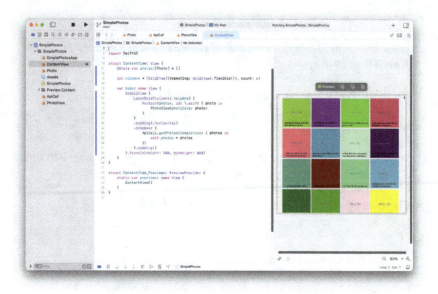

Figure 4-7 The preview of ContentView

Tada! This app is getting together, right? We can make more UI tweaks.

✖ Update **PhotoView** to only show text on mouseover.

PhotoView.swift

```swift
struct PhotoView: View {
  var photoData: Photo

  @State private var isOver = false

  var body: some View {
    ZStack(alignment: .bottom) {
      AsyncImage(url: URL(string: photoData.thumbnailUrl)) { image in
        image
          .resizable()
          .aspectRatio(contentMode: .fill)
      } placeholder: {
        Color.gray
      }.frame(width: 200, height: 200)

      if isOver {
        Text(photoData.title)
          .padding(5)
          .foregroundColor(.black)
          .frame(width: 200)
          .lineLimit(2)
      }
    }.onHover { isOver in
      self.isOver = isOver
    }
  }
}
```

```
}
```

You may notice some tweaks from the original PhotoView

- Add a **@State** variable called isOver

- Update this variable **isOver** when the mouse hovers the **ZStack**

- Show the title if **isOver** is true. Otherwise, don't render the title.

When you run the app, you can verify the hover behavior.

Figure 4-8 Run the app

✖ Implement the click behavior: when the photo is clicked, it opens a URL.

PhotoView.swift

```swift
import SwiftUI
```

```
struct PhotoView: View {
  var photoData: Photo

  @State private var isOver = false

  var body: some View {
    Link(destination: URL(string: photoData.url)!) {
      ZStack(alignment: .bottom) {
        AsyncImage(url: URL(string: photoData.thumbnailUrl)) { image in
          image
            .resizable()
            .aspectRatio(contentMode: .fill)
        } placeholder: {
          Color.gray
        }.frame(width: 200, height: 200)

        if isOver {
          Text(photoData.title)
            .padding(5)
            .foregroundColor(.black)
            .frame(width: 200)
            .lineLimit(2)
        }
      }.onHover { isOver in
        self.isOver = isOver
      }
    }
  }
}
```

To make the photo clickable, **Link()** now wraps the original **ZStack**.

When you run the app and click any photo in the app, it should immediately open a new URL in Safari.

That's it! A pretty basic photo viewer is complete.

✖ Run the app, and scroll through the photos.

You can see the photos are lazy loaded into the app. To verify the network calls are indeed triggered on demand, open the debug navigator, and click the Network tab.

As you scroll through, you can see the receiving and sending rates being positive in Figure 4-9.

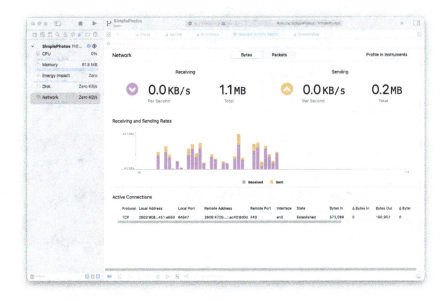

Figure 4-9 Receiving and Sending Rates are positive when you scroll through the photos in the app

❖ Tip

Debug Navigator is a very effective way to help evaluate the performance of your app.

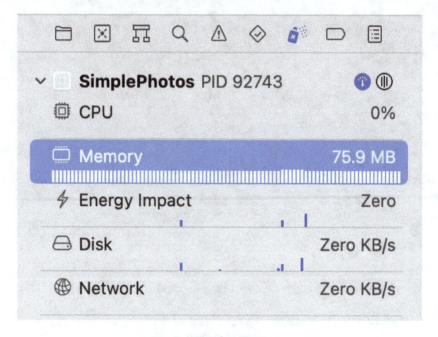

Figure 4-10 Debug Navigator

When your app is running in Xcode, you can check the **Memory** tab. It shows the current memory usage. If the usage is too high, it may trigger a warning. The app would risk termination if the memory usage enters the red area.

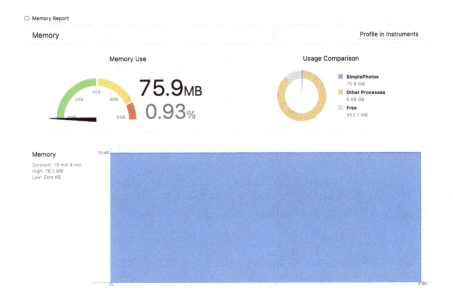

Figure 4-11 *Memory Report of the app*

When your app appears to have high memory usage, you can see whether the following are the root causes, and fix them or optimize them accordingly.

- Memory leaks

- Heavy animations

- Image assets are too large

- The size of Core Data transactions is too big

- Unused views being used

FULL CODE

You can find the code on Github: https://github.com/higracehuang/macos-app-simple-photos

CHAPTER 5: MACOS DEVELOPMENT AND SWIFTUI BASICS

"I hear and I forget. I see and I remember. I do and I understand." —
Confucius

We have built 3 macOS projects together. What do you think? Do you
feel more confident in building your ideas with macOS apps? If not, it is
okay.

In this chapter, we will go through the key concepts we have
encountered in the projects, so you can understand why and how they
are being used.

VIEWS

Views are the basic building blocks in SwiftUI. Each view is a struct.

Let's use **ContentView.swift** as an example.

```swift
import SwiftUI

struct ContentView: View {
  var body: some View {
    Text("Hello, world!")
      .padding()
  }
}
```

ContentView is a view because it conforms to the **View** protocol. What
is a **View** protocol? It defines a computed **body** property, which consists
of the contents and behavior of the view.

We can categorize views into 2 types: primitive views and container
views.

PRIMITIVE VIEWS

The primitive views are the most basic building blocks in the more complex custom views. You may have seen and used these primitive views in the early chapters.

Here are some examples of primitive views:

- Text()

- Image()

- Color()

- Shape()

- Spacer()

- Divider()

CONTAINER VIEWS

Container Views are for grouping and repeating views. Some are used to structure and layout, for example, stack views and grid views. Some are used to the more complex interfaces, such as lists and forms.

Here are some common Container Views:

- Pane()

- VStack()

- HStack()

- ScrollView()

- NavigationView()

- List()

- Form()

- LazyVGrid()

- LazyHGrid()

VIEW INSTANCE METHODS

View instance methods are used to configure a view. For example, if we would like to change the text color to red, we will add a method called **foregroundColor()**. To make the text bold, we will add the method **bold()**.

```
struct ContentView: View {
  var body: some View {
    Text("Hello, world!")
      .foregroundColor(.red)
      .bold()
  }
}
```

Each kind of view has a rich set of applicable methods. They make SwiftUI very expressive.

MANAGING STATES IN SWIFTUI

SwiftUI provides a range of property wrappers to define how the data is observed, rendered, and transferred between views.

Property Wrappers

You must have seen the notations with @ in the projects, such as **@State** and **@ObservedObject**. They are property wrappers.

A proper wrapper is a type that wraps a given value to attach additional logic to it. What kind of additional logic is it? Let's talk about it one by one below.

@State

@State is a property wrapper. Its "additional logic" is to automatically make the view update when this state variable was changed.

Here is a code snippet we had in the project in Chapter 2.

```
struct NoteEntryView: View {
  var noteEntry: NoteEntry

  /// Define states to store values of the text inputs
  @State private var titleInput: String = ""
  @State private var contentInput: String = ""

  var body: some View {
    if let title = noteEntry.title,
      let content = noteEntry.content,
      let updatedAt = noteEntry.updatedAt {
```

```
NavigationLink {
  VStack {
    /// Text field for Title. One-line Text Input.
    TextField("Title", text: $titleInput)
    /// When the view is rendered,
    /// update the text input with the fetched result.
      .onAppear() {
        self.titleInput = title
      }
    /// Text Editor for Content. Multi-line Text Input.
    TextEditor(text: $contentInput)
      .onAppear() {
        self.contentInput = content
      }
  }
} label: {
  Text(title)
  Text(updatedAt, formatter: itemFormatter)
}
    }
  }
}
```

The two **@State** properties **titleInput** and **contentInput** are first assigned when **noteEntry** is passed into the view (**onAppear**). So a user can see the view updated with the values.

Also note that the **@State** properties are designed to contain simple values, such as booleans, integers, and strings. They are used to manage transients that only affect the UI, such as turning on a toggle button, or highlighting the state of a button. They are not designed to store complex data types, such as structs or classes.

❖ Tip

It is intended to keep the **@State** properties **private**. It ensures that they will only be mutated within the body of the view.

@Binding

A SwiftUI view may consist of multiple child views. If you want to notify the child views when a variable in the parent view changes, at the same time notify the parent view when child views change, you can use **@Binding** variables.

In addition, **@Binding** variables are either primitive values, such as integers and strings, or any Swift data type.

```
import SwiftUI

struct ContentView: View {
  @State private var isSubAll:Bool = false
```

```
@State private var isSubNotif:Bool = false
@State private var isSubNews:Bool = false

var body: some View {
  VStack {
    Toggle("Subscribe All", isOn: $isSubAll)
      .onChange(of: isSubAll) { isSubAll in
        if isSubAll {
          isSubNotif = true
          isSubNews = true
        }
      }
    DetailedSubscriptionView(
      isSubNotif: $isSubNotif,
      isSubNews: $isSubNews)
  }.padding()
  }
}

struct DetailedSubscriptionView: View {
  @Binding var isSubNotif: Bool
  @Binding var isSubNews: Bool
  var body: some View {
    VStack {
      Toggle("Subscribe Notifications", isOn: $isSubNotif)
      Toggle("Subscribe News", isOn: $isSubNews)
    }
  }
}
```

In this example above, when the **@State** variable **isSubAll** changes to true, the **isSubNotif** and **isSubNews** will be changed to **true**. Because they are @Binding variables in the child view **DetailedSubscriptionView**, the toggles will change accordingly to be **on**.

Note that, when a **@Binding** variable is passed to a child view, this variable has a prefix $, for example, **$isSubNotif**. It is not an intrinsic value of the variable, such as Boolean. A binding value is like a vehicle that carries the state of the variable.

@EnvironmentObject

If you want a variable to be available for a view hierarchy (a tree of views), instead of passing the variable around, you can use an @EnvironmentObject.

```
import SwiftUI

class TweetSettings:ObservableObject {
  @Published var fontColor: Color = .blue
  @Published var picSize: CGFloat = 200
}

struct ContentView: View {
  var tweetSettings = TweetSettings()
  var body: some View {
    VStack {
```

```
      TweetView()
      TweetView()
      TweetView()
    }.environmentObject(tweetSettings)
  }
}

struct TweetView: View {
  var body: some View {
    ProfilePicView()
    TweetText()
  }
}

struct ProfilePicView: View {
  @EnvironmentObject var tweetSettings:TweetSettings
  var body: some View {
    Image(systemName: "bird")
      .resizable()
      .frame(
        width: tweetSettings.picSize,
        height: tweetSettings.picSize)
  }
}

struct TweetText: View {
  @EnvironmentObject var tweetSettings:TweetSettings
  var body: some View {
    Text("Tweet Text")
      .foregroundColor(tweetSettings.fontColor)
      .onTapGesture {
        tweetSettings.picSize = 150
      }
  }
}
```

In this example, the **tweetSettings** is passed as an **environmentObject** in **ContentView**. When it is needed in the child views at any level, we just need to declare it as **@EnvironmentObject** to get access to this variable.

If any attribute of this object (for example, **fontColor** or **picSize**) is changed, any view that has declared **tweetSettings** as **@EnvironmentObject** will invalidate the view and cause it to re-render.

In the example above, when the user taps on the **TweetText**, **picSize** is changed to **150**. It will notify all the instances of **ProfilePicView** to change the size because in **ProfilePicView** declares **TweetSettings** as **@EnvironmentObject**.

You can see, for **TweetText** and **ProfilePicView**, we do not pass the **tweetSettings** around. Instead, we declare it as **@EnvironmentObject** in any view that needs it.

Note that, **@EnvironmentObject** needs to work with **ObservableObject** variables. In another word, the model of

@EnvironmentObject should conform to the **ObservableObject** protocol.

@Environment

@Environment variables manage system-managed environment values, such as color schemes, whether the app is running in the light or dark mode, Core Data's managed object context (as mentioned in Chapter 2), etc. They are key-value pairs, and keys are predefined.

```
import SwiftUI

struct ContentView: View {
  @Environment(\.colorScheme) var colorScheme: ColorScheme

  var body: some View {
    VStack {
      Text(colorScheme == .light ? "Light Mode" : "Dark Mode")
    }
  }
}
```

The above code will check the system's predefined environment variable **colorScheme**. If it is **.light**, it will output **Light Mode**. Otherwise, it outputs **Dark Mode**.

Besides colorScheme, there are many other variables, such as **timeZone**(the current time zone that views should use when handling dates).

For the complete environment variables, you can refer to https://developer.apple.com/documentation/swiftui/environmentvalues.

@ObservedObject and @StateObject

If you want to pass an object to the view, and always get notified and re-render the view when the object changes, you can use **@ObservedObject**.

If you want to create an object inside the view, and re-render the view when the object changes, you can use **@StateObject**.

To illustrate the difference between **@ObservedObject** and **@StateObject**, this is an example slightly modified from the previous example with **@EnvironmentObject**. It achieves the same result as the example above: when the **TweetText** is clicked, the size of the **ProfilePicView** changes.

```
import SwiftUI
```

```
class TweetSettings:ObservableObject {
  @Published var fontColor: Color = .blue
  @Published var picSize: CGFloat = 200
}

struct ContentView: View {
  @StateObject var tweetSettings = TweetSettings()
  var body: some View {
    VStack {
      TweetView(tweetSettings: tweetSettings)
      TweetView(tweetSettings: tweetSettings)
      TweetView(tweetSettings: tweetSettings)
    }
  }
}

struct TweetView: View {
  @ObservedObject var tweetSettings:TweetSettings
  var body: some View {
    ProfilePicView(tweetSettings: tweetSettings)
    TweetText(tweetSettings: tweetSettings)
  }
}

struct ProfilePicView: View {
  @ObservedObject var tweetSettings:TweetSettings
  var body: some View {
    Image(systemName: "bird")
      .resizable()
      .frame(
        width: tweetSettings.picSize,
        height: tweetSettings.picSize)
  }
}

struct TweetText: View {
  @ObservedObject var tweetSettings:TweetSettings
  var body: some View {
    Text("Tweet Text")
      .foregroundColor(tweetSettings.fontColor)
      .onTapGesture {
        tweetSettings.picSize = 150
      }
  }
}
```

Note that, both **@ObservedObject** and **@StateObject** need to work
with **ObservableObject** variables.

CORE DATA

Core Data is the framework to manage data model objects in the app. It
is more than just SQLite data stores. It manages complex object graphs.
The data models in Core Data are called entities. In your app execution,
you can ask Core Data for filtered, sorted sets of entities for your needs.
The saved data is persistent, meaning that after the device or the app
restarts, data still exists.

In Chapter 2, we used Core Data to store the data locally. The capabilities of Core Data are far beyond managing local data. It can also sync data to multiple devices with CloudKit.

If you are an Apple Watch user, you may be familiar with the Activity app where you can see the exciting progress your connections are making (Figure 5-1). This is a perfect example of using Core Data to selectively share data with recipients.

Figure 5-1 Apple Watch app Activity

SF SYMBOLS

SF Symbols is a library of iconography designed to integrate seamlessly with San Francisco, the system font for Apple platforms. It is a collection of over 4,400 symbols (in SF Symbols 4, at the time of writing).

SF Symbols was introduced in 2019. This has been a big game changer for iOS and macOS developers. In the past, developers had to rely on 3rd party SVG icons.

SF Symbols App

To use SF Symbols, you don't need to include anything in your app project. They are already part of the OS system. All you need to do is to look up the names and version compatibility on the macOS SF Symbol app.

It can be downloaded here at https://developer.apple.com/sf-symbols/.

Figure 5-2 You can download SF Symbols on this website

How to Use SF Symbols

We used SF Symbols several times in the projects.

Here is one example from the Windowless Screenshot app.

Figure 5-3 The Menu in the status bar

To get appropriate icons, you just need to search in the SF Symbols app.

- For example, to the window icon, search **window** in the search bar.

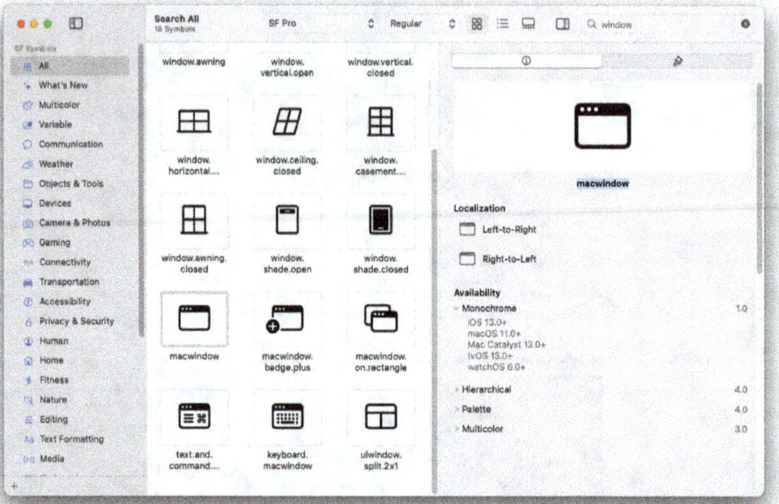

Figure 5-4 Details of the icon macwindow

- Find the icon you prefer, and click to see the details
- Check whether it is available in the target version (or above) of your app.
- If it is available for your target version, copy the string under the icon into the code. In this case, **macwindow**.

```
let windowImage = Image(systemName: "macwindow")
```

CHAPTER 6: PREPARING FOR LAUNCH

We have built 3 functional macOS apps together in the previous chapters. It is quite a milestone!

Before we finally package up the app and distribute it, we may still need some preparation, including:

• Minimum OS Version

• App Icon

• Localization

ADJUST THE MINIMUM OS VERSION

When I was developing RedacApp[5], the feedback that I received from customers was that they could not install the app, because their macOS versions were lower than the app's target version.

This is what one customer sent to me:

---

[5] https://gracehuang.gumroad.com/l/redac

Figure 6-1 A screenshot of a warning dialog that a customer sent me

Our goal is to distribute the app to the largest audience. Not all the customers have the versions that we have. Chances are your customers are using lower macOS versions.

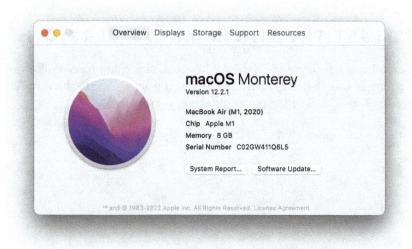

Figure 6-2 Go to Apple Icon→ About This Mac, you can find your macOS version. In this example, it is 12.2.1.

Build your code with a lower OS target and see what code breaks. Xcode will tell you what API is not available in what version. Based on the error messages, see whether you refactor the code to support the version.

- Select the project target notetaking in Xcode, and go to **General**. We can find the **Deployment Target** under **Deployment Info**.

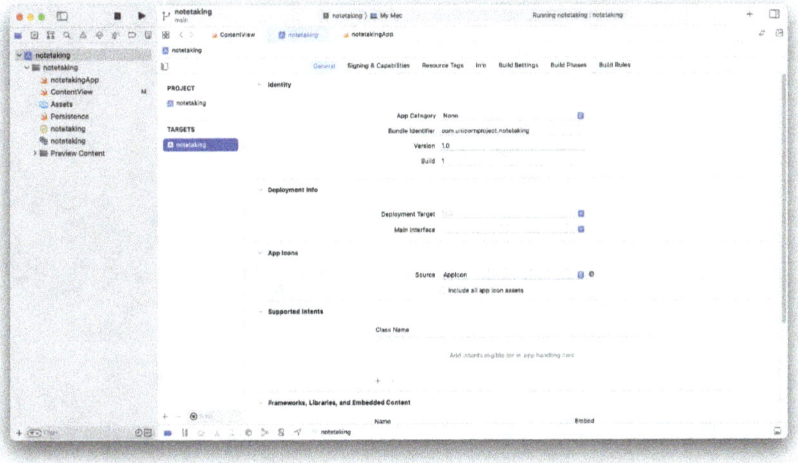

Figure 6-3 When we created the project, the Deployment Target was set to 12.2, which is the version of the Mac.

- Lower the **Deployment Target** gradually, and see whether you can still build the project.

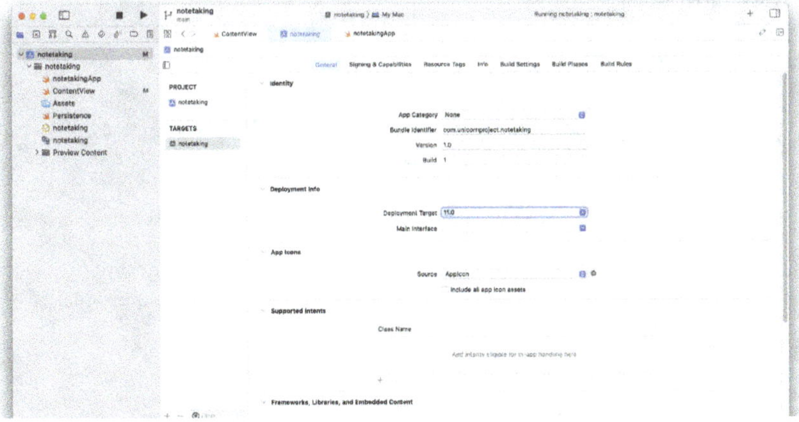

Figure 6-4 We lowered the Deployment Target to 11.0

APP ICON

At this point, without any app icons, the note-taking app should look like Figure 6-5.

Figure 6-5 The default blank app icon

Our goal is to design and create an icon for the note-taking app and apply it to the project.

App Icon Design

There are 3 ways to design app icons

- Hire professional designers

- Use online services

- Do it yourself

	Hire Professionals	Use online creative services	Do it yourself
Price	Cost more $$$	Reasonably priced $$	No cost $
Quality	High quality	Reasonably quality	Low quality (if you are not professional)
Flexibility	Flexible (Professionals design based on your preferences)	Less flexible (with limited options)	Flexible
How?	Hire contractors to do, or use	Use services like canva.com	Use existing tools, such as Figma, Photoshop, Gimp, etc.

❖ Tip

You can always iterate icons once you have the budget to improve them. If you don't have the budget yet, choose the low-cost approach.

For a successful app like Twitter, over the years, it took them many iterations to get to the current version, as shown in Figure 6-6.

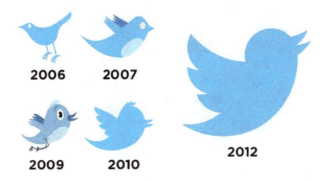

Figure 6-6 The evolution of Twitter logos

For example, we will use the logo in Figure 6-7 to illustrate the publishing process.

Figure 6-7 The app icon we will use

Generating App Icon Assets

This step takes an image and transforms it into a set of images that the Xcode project can use.

In the Project navigator, click the **Assets > AppIcon**, the 8 squares represent 8 different sizes of icons for different contexts.

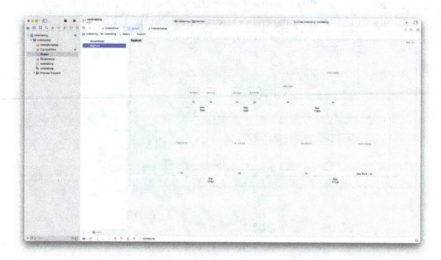

Figure 6-8 Before the app icons are configured

So, how can we create these images?

We can manually resize the source image of the app icon. But it would be time-consuming.

Fortunately, a lot of useful resources have already existed to solve this problem:

- AppIcon.co[6] – generating flat icons with different sizes. Useful for iOS apps, not macOS apps

- Image2Icon[7] - generating icons with rounded corners. Useful for macOS apps.

---

[6] https://appicon.co

[7] https://img2icnsapp.com

With the help of Image2Icon, I can generate an icon set, shown in Figure 6-9.

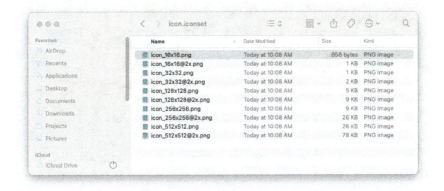

Figure 6-9 The icon set generated by Image2Icon

Updating the Project

✖ Drag the images into the right positions.

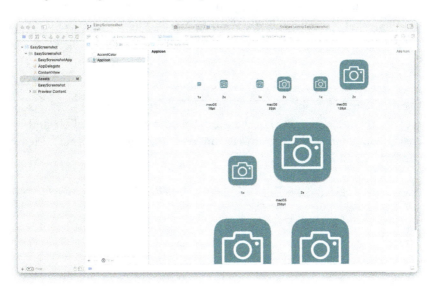

Figure 6-10 Placing the icons into the project based on the sizes

✖ Click Product > Clean Build Folder

■ Run the app

Figure 6-11 The look of the app icon in the dock

You can see the icon with a similar shape and similar size showing in the dock.

LOCALIZATION

Localization refers to a process of making your app support multiple languages. Your app will display in the user-specified language.

Usually, you first develop the app in the language of your primary users. In our case, it is English. If you want to expand the target users to other languages, you can add support for additional languages.

❖ Tip

Localization is optional. You don't need to do it if your customer base only needs one language. Localization can cost substantial effort and special language skills (e.g. translating one language to another). Please consider carefully before taking action in localization.

■ Go to **Project** > Under **Info** > Under **Localizations** > Click + to add a new language.

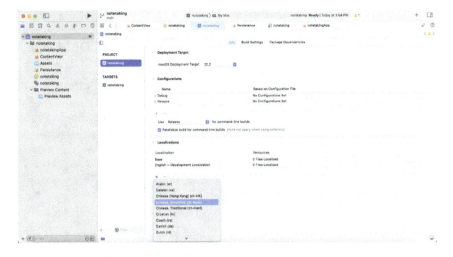

Figure 6-12 Choose Chinese, Simplified to localize

✖ Create a **Strings** File, via **File** > **New** > **File…**

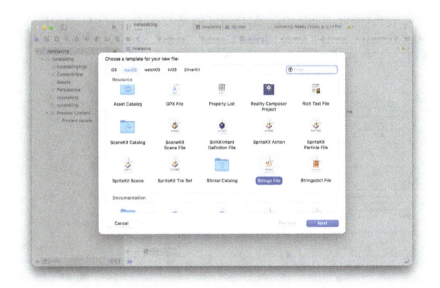

Figure 6-13 Creating a Strings file

✖ Click the **Localize…** button in the right pane under **Localization**.

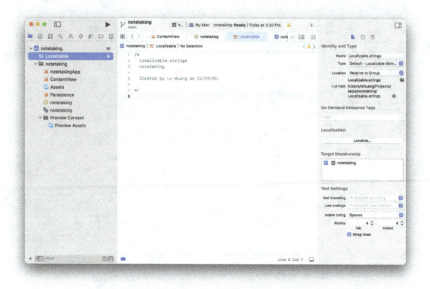

Figure 6-14 With the Strings file open, you can see Localize... button

You will see the dialog in Figure 6-15. In the dialog, you can choose what language to localize with. In this example, we choose English and Chinese (Simplified).

Figure 6-15 The dialog asking which language to localize

After you add all the languages you need to localize, you can see a list of languages on the right pane.

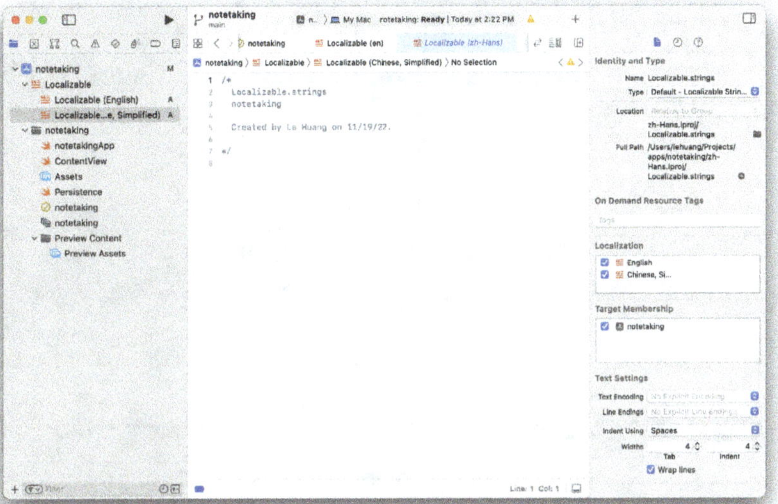

Figure 6-16 Two languages (English and Simplified Chinese)

- Find the strings that are used in the code. Take the note-taking app as an example.

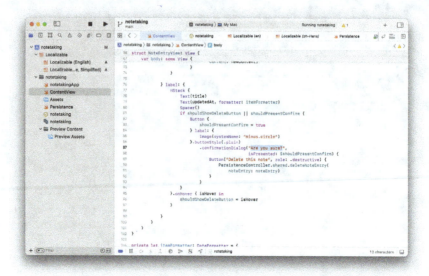

Figure 6-17 Finding the text that is used in the code

✖ Turn the text strings into key-value pairs in the Strings file.

Localizable (English)

```
"delete_question" = "Are you sure?";
"delete_confirm" = "Delete this note";
```

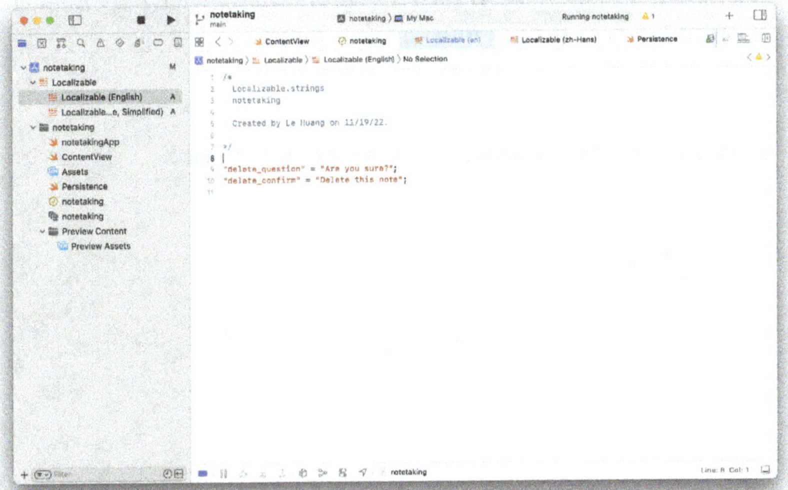

Figure 6-18 Setting up the English string translations

- Replace the text strings in the code with the keys in the **Localizable (English)**.

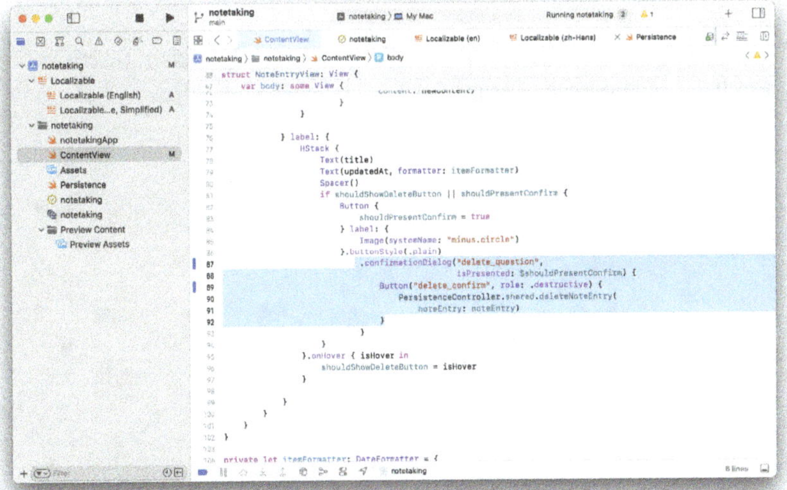

Figure 6-19 Replaced the human-readable text with a string

At this point, you've finished the localization for one langue - English. We can continue to localize for other languages.

✖ Create key-value pairs for other languages.

Figure 6-20 Setting up the Simplified Chinese string translations

✖ Run the app to confirm the base language. In this example, it is English, as shown in Figure 6-21.

Figure 6-21 Running app in an English environment

✖ Test running the app with other languages. Click **Edit Scheme** > **Options** > **App Language** > Choose **Chinese, Simplified** > **Close**.

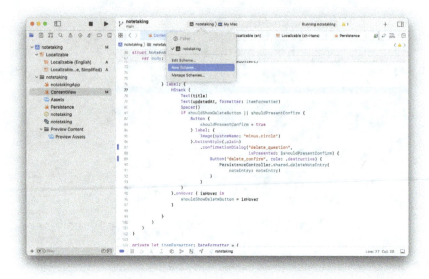

Figure 6-22 Choose Edit Scheme... to change the language environment

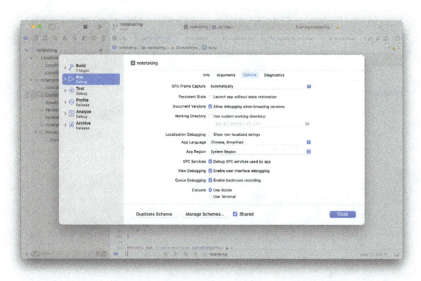

Figure 6-23 Change the App Language to Chinese, Simplified

Please note that this change is in the debugging settings, which will not be changed to the app. This is to mimic a user using the app in their local environment with their specified language.

✪ Now, run the app again, and you should be able to see the text has changed.

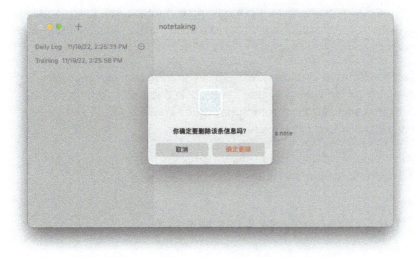

Figure 6-24 Run the app in the Simplified Chinese environment

Voila! The dialog is showing Simplified Chinese instead.

You may notice that, even though we did not purposely change the button text, the button text is still displayed in Chinese. It is because they are part of the standard components in SwiftUI.

CHAPTER 7: APP STORE

Unlike iOS apps which you can only distribute via App Store, you can distribute your macOS apps in two ways: self-distribution and App Store.

Self-distribution is more flexible, but you have to make your app available for download yourself and market yourself. App Store takes a cut (around 30%) from your app revenue and has a rigid and longer review, but it helps reach a bigger audience.

You choose one, or both of the two ways. In this chapter and the next, we will talk about two kinds of distribution methods.

VERSION MANAGEMENT

Once we publish an app, we will add more features or fix bugs over time. Version management is used to differentiate these incremental changes.

There are two definitions of versions in Xcode: **Version** number and **Build** number. Let's dive deep into how to define and use them for your app.

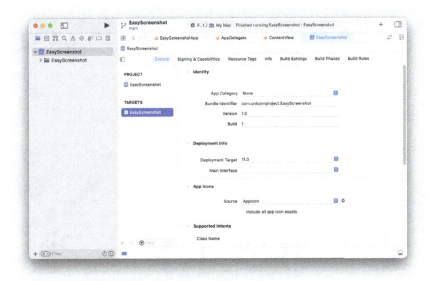

Figure 7-1 The Version and Build numbers are listed under General

Version Numbers

A version number is a name for each release of your app. For example, version 1.0.0 is the first release, while version 2.0.1 is the second release.

Apps on App Store follow semantic versioning conventions. The format is {major}.{minor}.{patch}. Major, minor, and patch are in numbers, which increment in the events of changes.

- Major number increments when you make incompatible API changes

- Minor number increments when you add functionality in a backward-compatible manner

- Patch number increments when you make backward-compatible bug fixes

The version you specify for the app will show up in the App Store for customers.

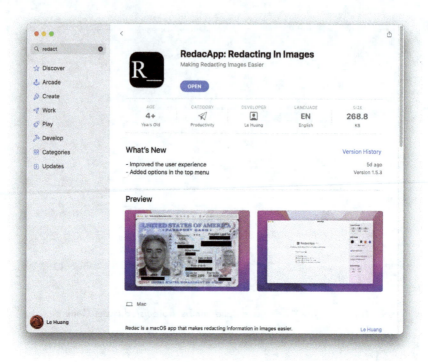

Figure 7-2 See the Version 1.5.3. It is published in App Store

In Xcode, the version is defined under **General** > (your build target) > **Identity -> Version**. For example, 1.1.0.

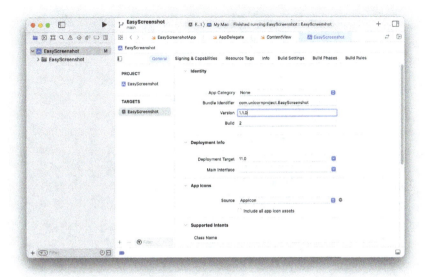

Figure 7-3 Changing the Version number to 1.1.0

In the code, the version is defined as **MARKETING_VERSION** in **project.pbxproj**. For example, in Figure 7-4. Please note that, as long as you make the change in Xcode, you don't need to separately make changes in **project.pbxproj**.

```
● ● ●  📄 EasyScreenshot — vi EasyScreenshot.xcodeproj/project.pbxproj — vi — vi EasyScreenshot.xcodeproj/project.pbxproj — 125×38
                            PRODUCT_BUNDLE_IDENTIFIER = com.unicornproject.EasyScreenshot;
                            PRODUCT_NAME = "$(TARGET_NAME)";
                            SWIFT_EMIT_LOC_STRINGS = YES;
                            SWIFT_VERSION = 5.0;
                    };
                    name = Debug;
            };
            06F206E829103C270073B4A6 /* Release */ = {
                    isa = XCBuildConfiguration;
                    buildSettings = {
                            ASSETCATALOG_COMPILER_APPICON_NAME = AppIcon;
                            ASSETCATALOG_COMPILER_GLOBAL_ACCENT_COLOR_NAME = AccentColor;
                            CODE_SIGN_ENTITLEMENTS = EasyScreenshot/EasyScreenshot.entitlements;
                            CODE_SIGN_STYLE = Automatic;
                            COMBINE_HIDPI_IMAGES = YES;
                            CURRENT_PROJECT_VERSION = 2;
                            DEVELOPMENT_ASSET_PATHS = "\"EasyScreenshot/Preview Content\"";
                            ENABLE_PREVIEWS = YES;
                            GENERATE_INFOPLIST_FILE = YES;
                            INFOPLIST_KEY_NSHumanReadableCopyright = "";
                            LD_RUNPATH_SEARCH_PATHS = (
                                    "$(inherited)",
                                    "@executable_path/../Frameworks",
                            );
                            MACOSX_DEPLOYMENT_TARGET = 11.0;
                            MARKETING_VERSION = 1.1.0;
                            PRODUCT_BUNDLE_IDENTIFIER = com.unicornproject.EasyScreenshot;
                            PRODUCT_NAME = "$(TARGET_NAME)";
                            SWIFT_EMIT_LOC_STRINGS = YES;
                            SWIFT_VERSION = 5.0;
                    };
                    name = Release;
            };
/* End XCBuildConfiguration section */

/* Begin XCConfigurationList section */
            06F206D229103C240073B4A6 /* Build configuration list for PBXProject "EasyScreenshot" */ = {
```

Figure 7-4 How the Version number is being managed in the code

Build

When you are preparing for a new release for your app, there could be issues that you need to address, for example, small bugs that you want to fix before the release, small tweaks on the strings, etc.

In this case, since you haven't released the app yet, you don't want to increment the version number. To differentiate these little changes, use the Build number.

In Xcode, the version is defined under **General** > (your build target) > **Identity -> Build**. For example, 2.

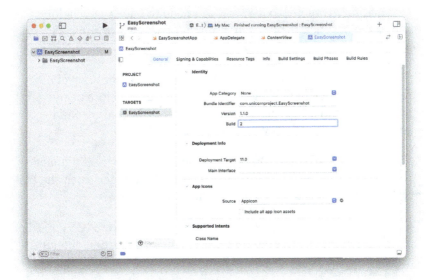

Figure 7-5 Changing the Build number in Xcode

In the code, the build is defined as **CURRENT_PROJECT_VERSION**
in **project.pbxproj**. For example:

```
                          PRODUCT_BUNDLE_IDENTIFIER = com.unicornproject.EasyScreenshot;
                          PRODUCT_NAME = "$(TARGET_NAME)";
                          SWIFT_EMIT_LOC_STRINGS = YES;
                          SWIFT_VERSION = 5.0;
               };
               name = Debug;
        };
        06F206E829103C27007384A6 /* Release */ = {
               isa = XCBuildConfiguration;
               buildSettings = {
                          ASSETCATALOG_COMPILER_APPICON_NAME = AppIcon;
                          ASSETCATALOG_COMPILER_GLOBAL_ACCENT_COLOR_NAME = AccentColor;
                          CODE_SIGN_ENTITLEMENTS = EasyScreenshot/EasyScreenshot.entitlements;
                          CODE_SIGN_STYLE = Automatic;
                          COMBINE_HIDPI_IMAGES = YES;
                          CURRENT_PROJECT_VERSION = 2;
                          DEVELOPMENT_ASSET_PATHS = "\"EasyScreenshot/Preview Content\"";
                          ENABLE_PREVIEWS = YES;
                          GENERATE_INFOPLIST_FILE = YES;
                          INFOPLIST_KEY_NSHumanReadableCopyright = "";
                          LD_RUNPATH_SEARCH_PATHS = (
                                   "$(inherited)",
                                   "@executable_path/../Frameworks",
                          );
                          MACOSX_DEPLOYMENT_TARGET = 11.0;
                          MARKETING_VERSION = 1.1.0;
                          PRODUCT_BUNDLE_IDENTIFIER = com.unicornproject.EasyScreenshot;
                          PRODUCT_NAME = "$(TARGET_NAME)";
                          SWIFT_EMIT_LOC_STRINGS = YES;
                          SWIFT_VERSION = 5.0;
               };
               name = Release;
        };
/* End XCBuildConfiguration section */

/* Begin XCConfigurationList section */
        06F206D229103C240073B4A6 /* Build configuration list for PBXProject "EasyScreenshot" */ = {
```

Figure 7-6 How the Build number is being managed in the code

Note that, for every new build, you will need to have a new build number greater than the last build number you used (for that same version).

For macOS apps, you must choose a new build number for every submission that is unique and has never been used before in any submission you have provided to the App Store (including build numbers used in previous versions of your app).

For example, for your macOS app, you can have 1.0.0 (build 1), and 1.0.0 (build 2). When you release 1.1.0, you should increment the build number as well. So the app will be named 1.1.0 (build 3).

The naming convention for macOS apps is different from iOS apps. For iOS apps, you may re-use build numbers when submitting different versions. For example, for your iOS app, you can have 1.0.0 (build 1), and 1.0.0 (build 2). When you release 1.1.0, you don't need to increment the build number as well. So the app will be named 1.1.0 (build 1).

If the convention for macOS apps is violated, you may not be able to upload to App Connect properly.

This is something that people who have prior experience in iOS development and the release cycle need to be aware of.

How to Use Build and Version

Now you are familiar with what Version and Build are, here are the steps to follow:

✖ Increment the **Version** number in Xcode.

✖ Increment the **Build** number in Xcode.

✖ (Optional) Git tag the code change.

As a best practice, we can also track the version changes in the Git history. For example,

```
git tag release-1.0.1
```

If you have a remote Git repo, you can follow the above command with this, to push it to the remote:

```
git push --tags
```

UPLOADING TO APP STORE

Now, let's get ready to upload the app to App Store.

✖ **Archive** the app.

Figure 7-7 Xcode > Product > Archive

Once the archive is ready, the following window will show up. Click **Distribute App**.

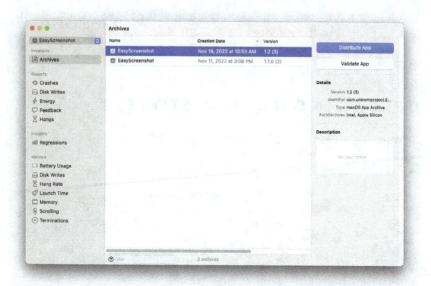

Figure 7-8 Archives

❖ **Tip**

In case you don't want to create an archive but still want to see the window above, you can go to **Xcode** > **Window** > **Organizer**.

✖ Choose **App Store Connect.**

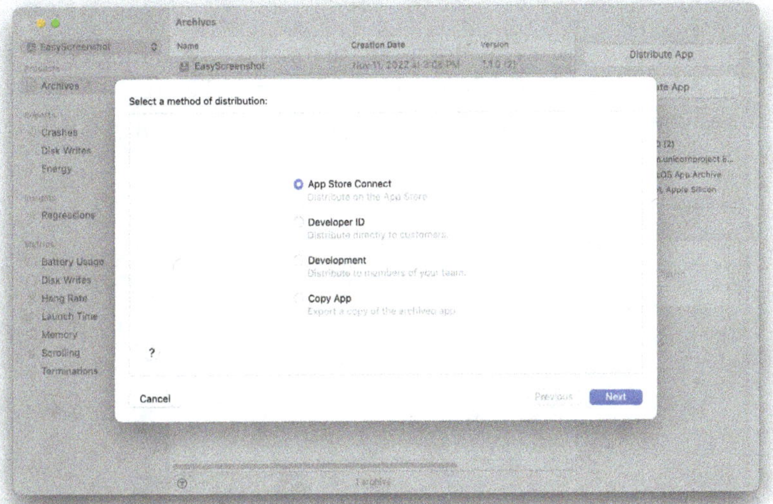

Figure 7-9 Choose App Store Connect

■ Choose **Upload.**

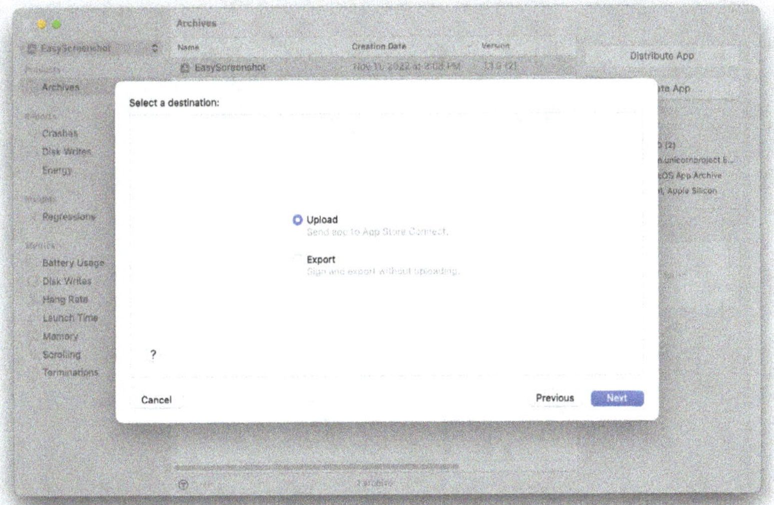

Figure 7-10 Choose Upload

✖ Choose a **Development Team** if no team is selected before.

If you did not choose a **Development Team** at the beginning of the project, it may ask you to choose one, as shown in Figure 7-11. This requires you to be a member of the Apple Developer Program, which is mentioned in Chapter 1.

Figure 7-11 Select a Development Team

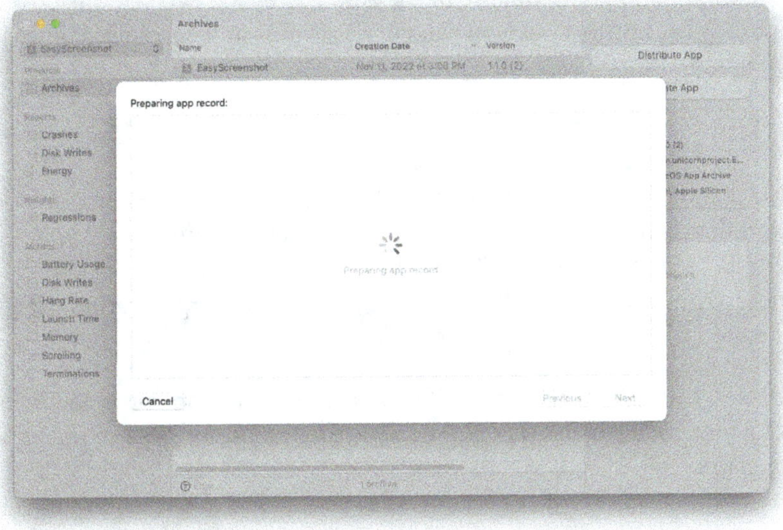

Figure 7-12 Once you click Next, it will start preparing app record

■ Confirm the information before submission.

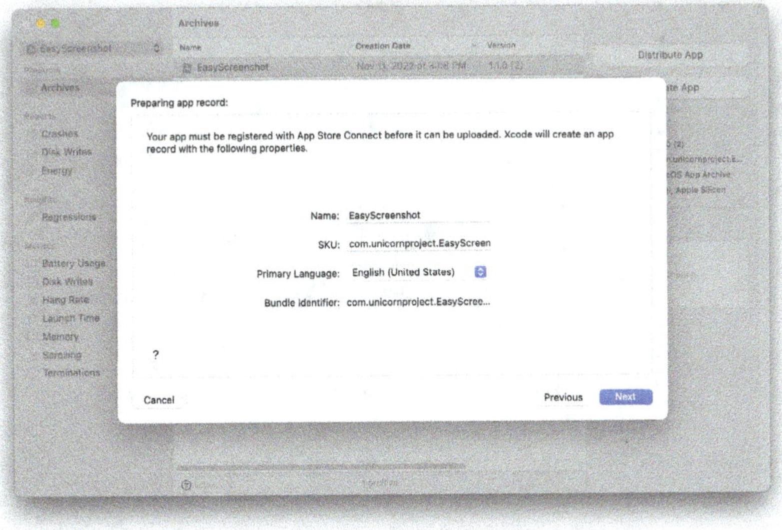

Figure 7-13 Confirm the information before submission

If the app name is not unique in the App Store, you can see this error in Figure 7-14. In this case, you can click Previous and consider a different app name.

❖ Tip

SKU stands for Stock Keeping Unit. It is a unique ID for your app in App Store that is not seen by users. You can use letters, numbers, hyphens, periods, and underscores. The SKU can't start with a hyphen, period, or underscore. Use a value that is meaningful to your organization. Can't be edited after saving the app record.

You don't need to change SKU if you encounter an app name collision, as long as the SKU itself is unique. The SKU does not have to match the app name.

Figure 7-14 The error shows not unique name in App Store

✖ Confirm the distribution options, and click **Next.**

Figure 7-15 App Store Connect distribution options

✖ Confirm the signing option.

Figure 7-16 Signing options

If you choose **Automatically manage signing**, it will use your Team profile that you have selected for signing.

If you choose **Manually manage signing**, you will need to upload a provisioning profile from the local machine.

In our case, we will use **Automatically manage signing**.

- Do a final review and upload.

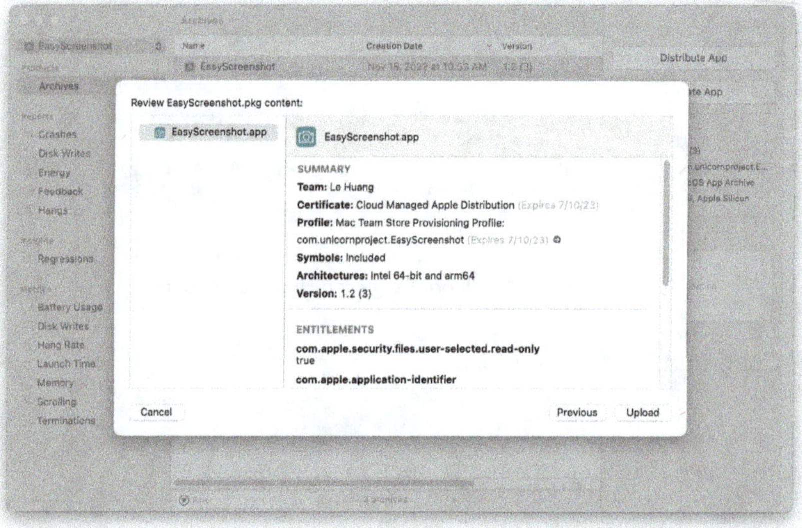

Figure 7-17 Review the app info before submission

Once the upload process is underway, you will see the window in Figure 7-18.

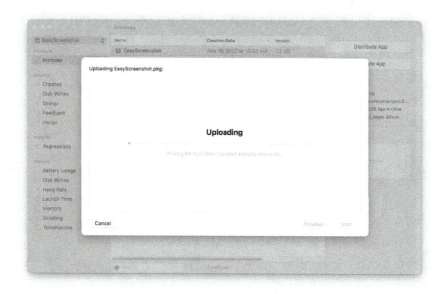

Figure 7-18 Uploading the app info and binary

Once the upload process is complete, you will see the confirmation in Figure 7-19.

Figure 7-19 Confirmation for successful upload

You can also see the app is being processed on App Store Connect.

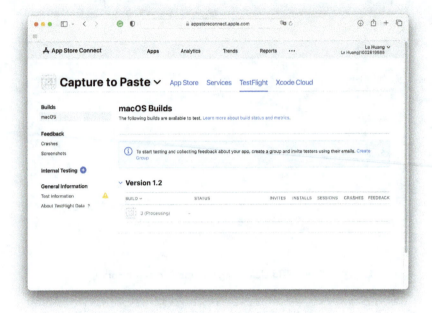

Figure 7-20 To view the uploaded builds on App Store Connect

Once the processing is complete, you may see the following screen in Figure 7-21.

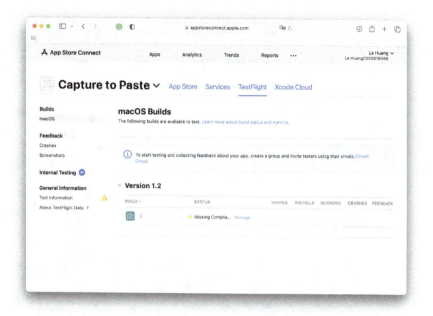

Figure 7-21 After the build upload is complete

The yellow warning sign **Missing Compliance** shown is a very common warning when you first submit your app to App Store. It is asking you to declare how you deal with user privacy data.

For this app, we don't send data to any external servers. There are two ways to resolve this warning. You could either manually click **Manage** to answer a series of questions whenever you upload a build (Figure 7-21), or configure in your project to declare the app's use of encryption. Obviously, the latter is more efficient.

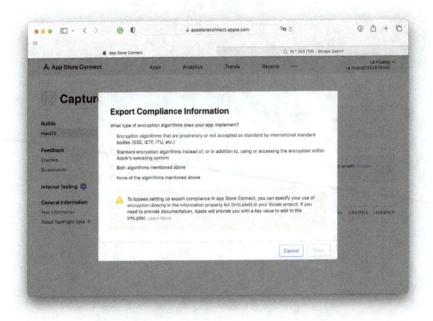

Figure 7-22 Resolving the compliance warning

DECLARE YOUR APP'S USE OF ENCRYPTION

It requires a file called Info.plist to declare your app's use of encryption. However, this file is not created by default.

✖ To create the Info.plist, go to **File** > **New** > **File...** > Choose **Property List** under **Resource** > Click **Next** -> Save As **Info** > Click **Create**. If you already have a .plist file, you can skip this step.

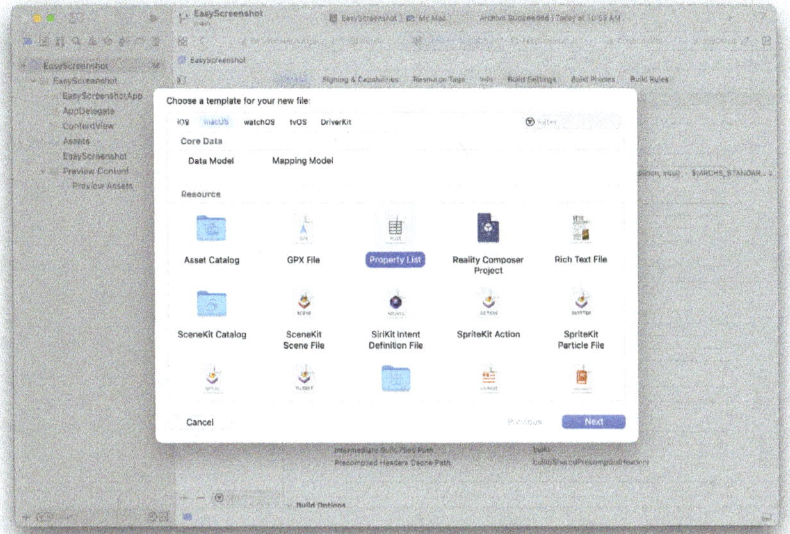

Figure 7-23 Creating a Property List file

- Link the newly created Info.plist, by going to **Build Settings** -> Search **Info.plist** > Fill the path with Info.plist.

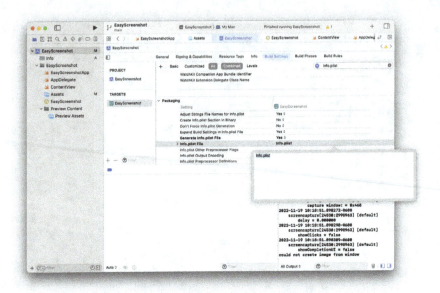

Figure 7-24 Link the .plist to the project

✖ Click on the **Info.plist** > right click **Information Property List** > type **App Uses Non-Exempt Encryption, boolean, No.**

In our case, we don't have any HTTP calls to any services. All data stays on the device. No encryption is needed.

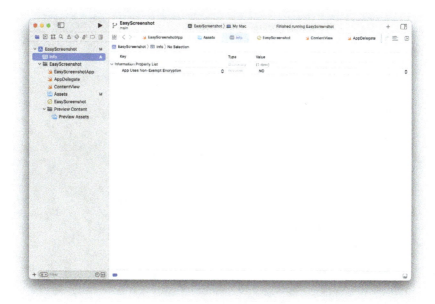

Figure 7-25 Declaring app uses no non-exempt encryption

❊ Update the **Build** number, build the project, and upload it to App Store. In the example, you can see this change in **Info.plist**, Build 4 has no such warning anymore.

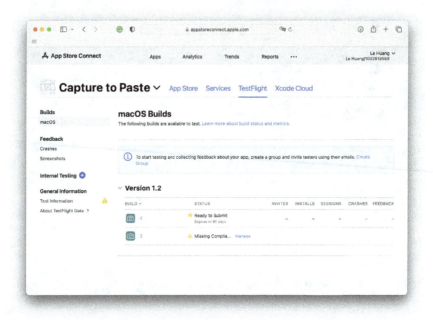

Figure 7-26 Build 4 has no missing compliance warning

REQUESTING FOR REVIEW

❌ To market your app in App Store, prepare appealing screenshots, and good copy for **Promotional Text**, **Description**, and **Keywords** on App Store Connect.

❌ Select the correct build, by clicking **Add Build**.

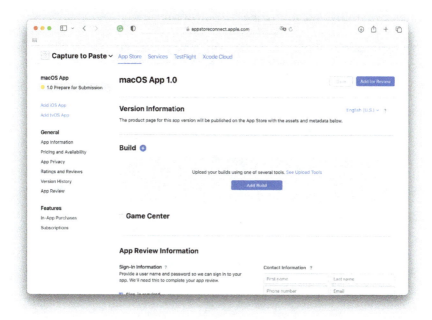

Figure 7-27 Select the build for submission

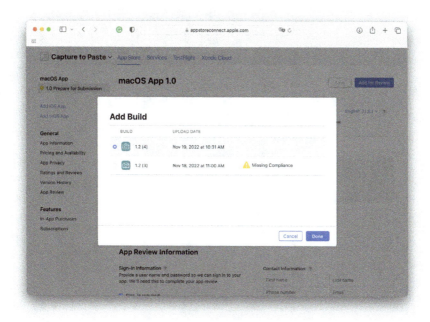

Figure 7-28 Choosing the build

After everything is ready, request Apple for review.

When the app is approved, Apple will send you an email. Usually, it takes about 1 to 2 days. Then your app is in the App Store! Congratulations!

CHAPTER 8: SELF-DISTRIBUTION

Apart from submitting to App Store, another way to distribute is distributing the app yourself.

NOTARIZE

If you distribute the installer yourself, how can your users trust something you build? Apple offers a notary service for your app.

The notarizing process is very quick — 2-3 minutes.

✖ **Archive** the app.

✖ Select **Distribute App.**

✖ Choose **Developer ID** (Figure 8-1) .

Figure 8-1 Select Developer ID

✖ Choose **Upload** (send to notary service) (Figure 8-2).

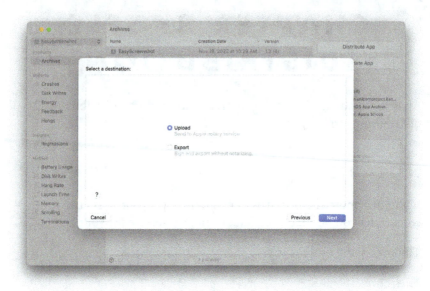

Figure 8-2 Choose to upload to Apple notary service

◈ Choose how you want to sign the app (Figure 8-3).

Figure 8-3 Choose automatically manage signing

✖ Click **Upload** (Figure 8-4).

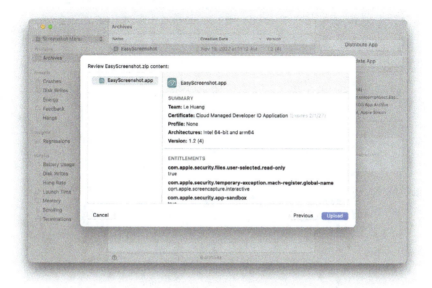

Figure 8-4 Review the app info before uploading it to notary service

✖ You will see a final confirmation page as shown in Figure 8-5.

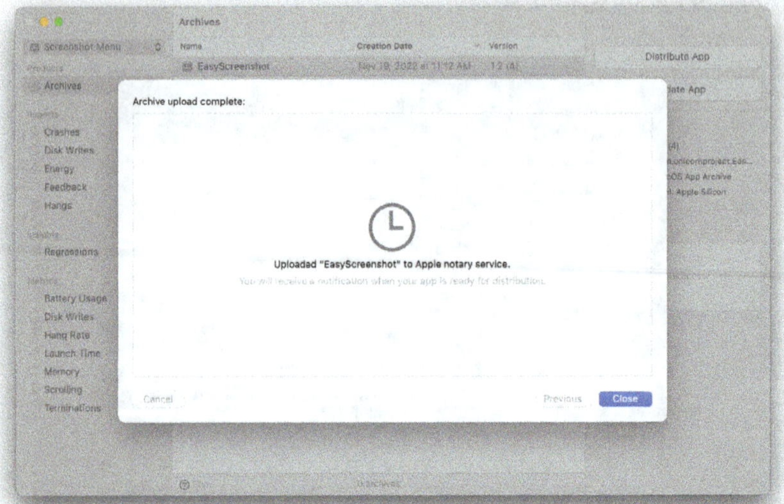

Figure 8-5 Upload confirmation

- Wait for a notification on Xcode with the title "Your Mac software was successfully notarized." Then your .app is ready to distribute. Click **Export Notarized App** to save the .app file to your preferred location.

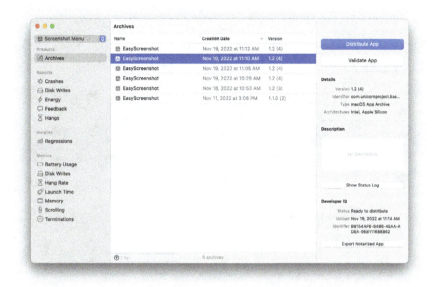

Figure 8-6 Once it is notarized, you can see the Export Notarized App button on the right

❖ Tip

Now, wonder why you have to pay Apple $99, even though you don't plan to sell your app in App Store? Yes, all the services, such as the notary service, and app reviews, are included in this price.

GENERATING INSTALLER

You could either hand over a .app file or a .dmg installer for your users.

But, what is the difference between .app and .dmg files?

.dmg is a copy of a virtual disk, which contains all the contents including a .app file, and maybe a README file. It also provides a process to install the app.

Figure 8-7 Opening the Installer

A .app file is a self-contained entity that has the necessary frameworks and libraries to function on its own. You can simply drag a .app file to the Applications folder to install the app.

To generate a .dmg file for the app, I often use create-dmg[8].

To make it easier before each release, I turn the script into a Shell script and save it together with the app source.

make-dmg.sh

```
create-dmg \
--volname "EasyScreenshot Installer" \
--window-pos 200 120 \
--window-size 800 400 \
--icon-size 100 \
--icon "EasyScreenshot.app" 200 190 \
--hide-extension "EasyScreenshot.app" \
--app-drop-link 600 185 \
"EasyScreenshot-Installer.dmg" \
"dist/"
```

MAKING APP AVAILABLE FOR DOWNLOAD

This step is to make the .dmg installer available for download.

---

[8] https://github.com/create-dmg/create-dmg

Here are a few options:

Option 1: Build a website and offer the download there.

Pros

Flexible: You could control the user experience on the website

Cons

Upfront and recurring cost and setup time: You would need to buy a domain, hosting on a cloud platform, and set up payment

Initial zero drive traffic: SEO and backlinks would be needed

Option 2: Use Creator Platforms (e.g. Gumroad)

Pros

No upfront cost: You just need to fill in the information and pricing. You will only be charged on a per-sale basis.

Cons

Initial zero drive traffic: You would need to market the product and backlink yourself.

Slightly less flexible: Compared to a custom-built website, you cannot change the website dramatically. However, in general, it meets all the needs.

Option 3: Upload it to a cloud drive (e.g. Google Drive, Dropbox)

Pros

No upfront or recurring cost.

Cons

Unable to set up payment: If you want to monetize on the app, this option would lack this functionality.

Initial zero drive traffic: You would need to backlink this app somewhere else, for example, in a blog post or on Twitter.

In my case, I find Gumroad awesome. Not only do you host the app for free there, but you can also keep a mailing list of the customers. Once you have updates to the app, you can inform them as well.

CONCLUSION

In this book, we have gone through the process of building macOS apps, the key basics of SwiftUI and macOS development, and the process of publishing macOS apps.

SwiftUI and macOS development will continue to evolve as Apple improves the ecosystem. I hope this book serves as a good point for learning about them.

For more advanced topics, here are good resources online.

Apple Developer Documentation: https://developer.apple.com/documentation/ (Great for API lookups)

Stack Overflow: https://stackoverflow.com/ (Great for problem-solving and examples)

AppCoda: https://www.appcoda.com/ (SwiftUI tutorials and courses)

Hacking With Swift: https://www.hackingwithswift.com/ (Good short articles about Swift)

Swift With Majid: https://swiftwithmajid.com/ (Good articles about Swift)

Ray Wenderlich: https://www.raywenderlich.com/ (Great tutorials about iOS and macOS development)

I hope at this point you are confident and motivated to build macOS apps by yourselves. I can't wait to see what you will build.

ABOUT AUTHOR

Grace Huang was a software engineer at several big tech companies, including Amazon, Bloomberg. Grace co-founded a hardware / AI company Roxy. The product line was later acquired and the team joined Twitter. Since leaving Twitter, Grace has been focusing on writing and teaching.

Other technical books that Grace wrote:

- Nail A Coding Interview: Six-Step Mental Framework

- Code Reviews In Tech: The Missing Guide

- A Practical Guide to Writing a Software Technical Design Document

- Dynamic Trio: Building Web Applications with React, Next.js & Tailwind

You can reach Grace at @imgracehuang on Twitter.

ABOUT REVIEWER

Han "Hannah" Zhang is a software engineer with 4+ years of experience building mobile and web applications. She works at Alto, a ride-share company, as a Front End Engineer.

Hannah holds an M.S. in Computer Science from Southern Methodist University and an M.S. in Electrical and Electronics Engineering from Soochow University.

www.ingramcontent.com/pod-product-compliance
Lightning Source LLC
LaVergne TN
LVHW051735050326
832903LV00023B/930